ClearRevise

AQA GCSE
English Literature

Illustrated revision and practice

Dr Jekyll and Mr Hyde
By Robert Louis Stevenson

Published by
PG Online Limited
The Old Coach House
35 Main Road
Tolpuddle
Dorset
DT2 7EW
United Kingdom

sales@pgonline.co.uk
www.clearrevise.com
www.pgonline.co.uk
2023

PREFACE

Absolute clarity! That's the aim.

This is everything you need to ace the question on *Dr Jekyll and Mr Hyde* and beam with pride. The content is laid out in a beautifully illustrated format that is clear, approachable and as concise and simple as possible.

The checklist on the contents pages will help you keep track of what you have already worked through and what's left before the big day.

We have included worked exam-style questions with answers. There is also an exam-style question at the end of the book. You can check your answer against that given on page 52.

LEVELS OF LEARNING

Based on the degree to which you are able to truly understand a new topic, we recommend that you work in stages. Start by reading a short explanation of something, then try to recall what you've just read. This will have limited effect if you stop there but it aids the next stage. Question everything. Write down your own summary and then complete and mark a related exam-style question. Cover up the answers if necessary but learn from them once you've seen them. Lastly, teach someone else. Explain the topic in a way that they can understand. Have a go at the different practice questions – they offer an insight into how and where marks are awarded.

Design and artwork: Jessica Webb / PG Online Ltd

First edition 2023   10 9 8 7 6 5 4 3 2 1
A catalogue entry for this book is available from the British Library
ISBN: 978-1-910523-92-6
Copyright © PG Online 2023
All rights reserved
No part of this publication may be reproduced, stored in a retrieval system, or transmitted in any form or by any means without the prior written permission of the copyright owner.

Printed on FSC® certified paper by Bell and Bain Ltd, Glasgow, UK.

THE SCIENCE OF REVISION

Illustrations and words

Research has shown that revising with words and pictures doubles the quality of responses by students.[1] This is known as 'dual-coding' because it provides two ways of fetching the information from our brain. The improvement in responses is particularly apparent in students when they are asked to apply their knowledge to different problems. Recall, application and judgement are all specifically and carefully assessed in public examination questions.

Retrieval of information

Retrieval practice encourages students to come up with answers to questions.[2] The closer the question is to one you might see in a real examination, the better. Also, the closer the environment in which a student revises is to the 'examination environment', the better. Students who had a test 2–7 days away did 30% better using retrieval practice than students who simply read, or repeatedly reread material. Students who were expected to teach the content to someone else after their revision period did better still.[3] What was found to be most interesting in other studies is that students using retrieval methods and testing for revision were also more resilient to the introduction of stress.[4]

Ebbinghaus' forgetting curve and spaced learning

Ebbinghaus' 140-year-old study examined the rate at which we forget things over time. The findings still hold true. However, the act of forgetting facts and techniques and relearning them is what cements them into the brain.[5] Spacing out revision is more effective than cramming – we know that, but students should also know that the space between revisiting material should vary depending on how far away the examination is. A cyclical approach is required. An examination 12 months away necessitates revisiting covered material about once a month. A test in 30 days should have topics revisited every 3 days – intervals of roughly a tenth of the time available.[6]

Summary

Students: the more tests and past questions you do, in an environment as close to examination conditions as possible, the better you are likely to perform on the day. If you prefer to listen to music while you revise, tunes without lyrics will be far less detrimental to your memory and retention. Silence is most effective.[5] If you choose to study with friends, choose carefully – effort is contagious.[7]

---

1. Mayer, R. E., & Anderson, R. B. (1991). Animations need narrations: An experimental test of dual-coding hypothesis. *Journal of Education Psychology*, (83)4, 484–490.
2. Roediger III, H. L., & Karpicke, J.D. (2006). Test-enhanced learning: Taking memory tests improves long-term retention. *Psychological Science*, 17(3), 249–255.
3. Nestojko, J., Bui, D., Kornell, N. & Bjork, E. (2014). Expecting to teach enhances learning and organisation of knowledge in free recall of text passages. *Memory and Cognition*, 42(7), 1038–1048.
4. Smith, A. M., Floerke, V. A., & Thomas, A. K. (2016) Retrieval practice protects memory against acute stress. *Science*, 354(6315), 1046–1048.
5. Perham, N., & Currie, H. (2014). Does listening to preferred music improve comprehension performance? *Applied Cognitive Psychology*, 28(2), 279–284.
6. Cepeda, N. J., Vul, E., Rohrer, D., Wixted, J. T. & Pashler, H. (2008). Spacing effects in learning a temporal ridgeline of optimal retention. *Psychological Science*, 19(11), 1095–1102.
7. Busch, B. & Watson, E. (2019), *The Science of Learning*, 1st ed. Routledge.

CONTENTS

Assessment objectives vi

Context, language and structure

Stevenson and *Dr Jekyll and Mr Hyde* 2
Context 4
Features of the novella 6
Language techniques 8

Analysis of acts

Chapter One: Story of the Door 11
Chapter Two: Search for Mr Hyde 13
Chapter Three: Dr Jekyll was Quite at Ease 15
Chapter Four: The Carew Murder Case 16
Chapter Five: Incident of the Letter 17
Chapter Six: Incident of Dr Lanyon 18
Chapter Seven: Incident at the Window 19
Chapter Eight: The Last Night 20
Chapter Nine: Dr Lanyon's Narrative 22
Chapter Ten: Henry Jekyll's Full Statement of the Case 24

Analysis of characters

Characters: Henry Jekyll / Edward Hyde 27
Characters: Gabriel Utterson 32
Characters: Hastie Lanyon 36
Characters: Richard Enfield & Poole 37

Analysis of themes

Themes: Dual nature .... 38 ☑
Themes: Reputation .... 42 ☐
Themes: Religion and Science .... 46 ☐
Themes: Secrecy .... 50 ☐
Examination practice **51**

Examination practice answers 52
Levels-based mark schemes for extended response questions 53
Index 54
Examination tips **57**

MARK ALLOCATIONS

All the questions in this book require extended responses. These answers should be marked as a whole in accordance with the levels of response guidance on **page 53**. The answers provided are examples only. There are many more points to make than there are marks available, so the answers are not exhaustive.

ASSESSMENT OBJECTIVES

In the exam, your answers will be marked against assessment objectives (AOs). It's important you understand which skills each AO tests.

AO1

- Show the ability to read, understand and respond to texts.
- Answers should maintain a critical style and develop an informed personal response.
- Use examples from the text, including quotes, to support and illustrate points.

AO2

- Analyse the language, form and structure used by a writer to create meanings and effects, using relevant subject terminology where appropriate.

AO3

- Show understanding of the relationships between texts and the contexts in which they were written.

AO4

- Use a range of vocabulary and sentence structures for clarity, purpose and effect, with accurate spelling and punctuation.

The AOs on this page have been written in simple language. See the AQA website for the official wording.

PAPER 1
Shakespeare and the 19th-century novel

Information about Paper 1

Written exam: 1 hour 45 minutes (this includes the question on Shakespeare)

64 marks (30 marks for Shakespeare plus 4 marks for SPaG, and 30 marks for the 19th-century novel)

40% of the qualification grade (20% each for Shakespeare and the 19th-century novel)

This guide covers the section on the 19th-century novel.

Questions
One extended-writing question per text

STEVENSON AND *DR JEKYLL AND MR HYDE*

Strange Case of Dr Jekyll and Mr Hyde is a novella by Robert Louis Stevenson.

Robert Louis Stevenson

Robert Louis Stevenson (1850–1894) was a novelist and poet, who often wrote stories and poems for children, such as *Treasure Island* and *Kidnapped*.

He was born and educated in Edinburgh and his family were very religious. As a young adult, he rejected religion and became an **atheist** (someone who doesn't believe in the existence of God). He was also interested in **bohemianism** (a socially unconventional lifestyle, with an interest in travel and the arts). Stevenson's family disapproved of his lifestyle choices.

> **Comment:** Stevenson's atheism influenced the events in *Strange Case of Dr Jekyll and Mr Hyde*. For more on the theme of religion, turn to **page 46**.

Robert Louis Stevenson

Stevenson wrote *Strange Case of Dr Jekyll and Mr Hyde* in 1886. He died eight years later in 1894, when he was only 44.

Dr Jekyll and Mr Hyde

Dr Jekyll and Mr Hyde is a novella: a short novel. It has elements of a **detective novel** and is an example of the **Gothic fiction** genre (see next page).

> The full title is *Strange Case of Dr Jekyll and Mr Hyde*, but we've shortened it to *Dr Jekyll and Mr Hyde* for simplicity.

Detective novel

Dr Jekyll and Mr Hyde borrows some features of detective novels:

 Detective novels usually have a twist at the end, for example, the murderer was the person the reader least expected. In *Dr Jekyll and Mr Hyde*, the twist is that Jekyll and Hyde are the same person.

 Detective stories usually feature a murder, and the detective must work out who committed the crime. In *Dr Jekyll and Mr Hyde*, several crimes are committed, and the reader knows who's responsible: Hyde. Instead, the mystery centres around who Hyde is, and how he's involved with Jekyll.

 The word 'case' in the title *Strange Case of Dr Jekyll and Mr Hyde* reminds the reader of case files used by detectives when they are investigating a crime.

Dr Jekyll and Mr Hyde continued

Gothic fiction

Dr Jekyll and Mr Hyde is an example of Gothic fiction (sometimes called Gothic horror), a genre of literature which was popular in the 19th century. Gothic fiction often included:

Other examples of Gothic fiction from this period include *Frankenstein* (1818) and *Dracula* (1897).

 Uneasy atmosphere: Gothic novels revolve around eerie and scary events. *Dr Jekyll and Mr Hyde* maintains an uneasy atmosphere up until the very end.

 Awful weather: In the novella, London is often foggy. The weather is also described as *"wild, cold"* and *"full of wind"*.

 A monster: Hyde commits terrible crimes, and his appearance is often described as being sub-human. He also behaves in a *"monstrous"* way.

 The supernatural: Jekyll uses *"transcendental"* (spiritual) science to become Hyde.

 Death: There are multiple deaths in the novella. Jekyll (along with Hyde) die, as well as Sir Danvers Carew and Lanyon.

 Suspense and mystery: Stevenson only reveals the final twist at the very end.

 A troubled protagonist: Jekyll is tormented by his wicked side and the actions of Hyde. For more on the theme of dual nature, turn to **page 38**.

 Plot points revealed through letters and diaries: The final two chapters consist entirely of letters from other characters. This is known as **epistolary** form.

Many Gothic fiction novels are set in remote, faraway places which helps to create a mysterious atmosphere. However, *Dr Jekyll and Mr Hyde* is set in London. This makes the novella even more unsettling because the events happen very close to home.

GCSE English Literature | Dr Jekyll and Mr Hyde

CONTEXT

The context of the Victorian period is important for understanding the deeper meaning of the story.

 You need to comment on context to get marks for AO3 (see **page vi**).

Setting

The year the story takes place is never confirmed, but it is likely to be around the time it was written (1886). The novella is set entirely in London.

Comment: *Dr Jekyll and Mr Hyde* combines elements of realism (i.e. setting the novella in London) with elements of the supernatural (i.e. transformative science). The elements of realism make the supernatural events of the novella seem more believable.

Class

British society in the 19th century could be categorised into three classes: upper, middle and working class. Upper-class families were the richest members of society and belonged to the aristocracy (families with inherited land and wealth). Upper-class families probably made up about 5% of the population.

Those in the middle class had money, but they earned it through respectable employment, such as medicine (like Dr Lanyon) or law (like Utterson). They accounted for approximately 15% of the population.

Fashionable London gentlemen strolling through a park.

Upper- and middle-class men were expected to act in a gentlemanly way. Gentlemen were supposed to be polite, moral and respectable. They avoided displays of strong emotion, and behaved in a reserved manner. Gentlemen were faithful Christians, who believed in God and attended church. They avoided 'sinful' behaviour such as drinking too much alcohol, having sex outside of marriage or indulging in anything that other gentlemen might disapprove of.

Being a gentleman provided access to influential social connections which were important for business, finding a suitable wife and earning the respect and admiration of others.

Gentlemen would take frequent walks through their local area, greeting other respectable families. This reminded people that they belonged to the social elite.

Comment: Utterson and Enfield go walking together every Sunday around London.

However, some gentlemen would secretly indulge in behaviour that was considered immoral or disgraceful. They might visit brothels to have sex outside of marriage; go to pubs to drink and gamble; or opium dens to smoke drugs.

Comment: Jekyll struggles with his dual nature. He wants to be a respectable gentleman, but he also wants to indulge in immoral behaviour without damaging his reputation. This pressure to be respectable forces him to create Hyde.

Religion

Most Victorians were Christians who believed in God, followed the teachings of the Bible and went to church every Sunday.

Comment: Religion is an important theme in the novella. For more detail, turn to **page 46**.

Many Victorian Christians believed in **creationism**: the idea that God created Earth and everything on it. Creationism was widely accepted because it was written in the Bible.

Comment: The Theory of Evolution (see below) contradicted creationism.

However, during the Victorian period, there was a greater focus on education and an increase in scientific knowledge. Certain scientific discoveries began to undermine what was taught in the Bible, which led some Victorians to reject Biblical interpretations of how the world was created.

Science

As technology advanced during the Victorian period (for example, improvements to microscopes), there were more scientific discoveries and greater public interest in science.

One of the most significant scientific developments in the 19th century was published in Charles Darwin's *On the Origin of Species* (1859). Darwin believed that animals had developed over time, and that humans had evolved from apes. Darwin's theory received a lot of criticism because it directly opposed creationism. Some people were also disturbed by the suggestion that mankind was descended from primitive, uncivilised animals.

A cartoon mocking Darwin.

Comment: Hyde is presented as less evolved than the other characters in the novella. He is often described as having animalistic traits and he exhibits *"ape-like"* fury.

People who believed in scientific theories which contradicted the Bible could be shunned by other members of society.

Comment: Lanyon disapproves of Jekyll's *"unscientific balderdash"*, and no longer wants to be associated with him. For more on the theme of science, turn to **page 46**.

Fin de siècle

Fin de siècle is a French phrase which means 'end of the century', but it also describes a feeling that some people felt towards the end of the 19th century. As the 1800s drew to a close, some people felt anxious about what the new century would bring. There had been a lot of changes in the 1800s in science, religion and society as a whole, and people felt uncertain about the future.

Comment: *Dr Jekyll and Mr Hyde* embodies this feeling of uncertainty, and the struggle between old-fashioned beliefs, and newer, more radical attitudes.

FEATURES OF THE NOVELLA

Dr Jekyll and Mr Hyde is a novella: a short novel.

Chapters

The novella has ten chapters. Stevenson gives each chapter a title (such as *Search for Mr Hyde*) rather than numbering them. These titles hint at what will happen in each chapter.

Narrator

Dr Jekyll and Mr Hyde mainly uses a third-person narrator and most of the novella is told from the perspective of Utterson. However, several important plot points are revealed by other characters.
- The account of Hyde trampling the girl is told by Enfield.
- A maid recalls Hyde murdering Sir Danvers Carew.
- Hyde's transformation into Jekyll is told through Lanyon's letter.

Comment: Since Utterson (and therefore the reader) doesn't witness these important events first-hand, Utterson is forced to investigate to try to discover the truth.

The final two chapters are told through letters: *Dr Lanyon's Narrative* and *Henry Jekyll's Full Statement of the Case*. These letters are written in the first person, which allow the reader to experience events from other characters' perspectives. They also reveal secrets which had been hidden from Utterson (and the reader) which help to resolve the events of the novella.

Comment: Telling parts of the story through letters also allows the reader to understand other characters' emotions and motivations. For example, in *Henry Jekyll's Full Statement of the Case*, Jekyll explains how tormented he was by his experiences with Hyde. This helps to create sympathy for Jekyll.

Structure

Most of the novella is set in Utterson's present. The story is **chronological**, with one significant leap in time: a year passes between *Dr Jekyll was Quite at Ease* and *The Carew Murder Case*.

Comment: The chronological structure means that the reader finds out information at the same time as Utterson, so they are more involved in the story.

The final two chapters, *Dr Lanyon's Narrative* and *Henry Jekyll's Full Statement of the Case*, recount events that took place in the past. These chapters help to fill in some gaps in the narrative (e.g. why Dr Lanyon is so weak in *Incident of Dr Lanyon*).

Comment: Telling parts of a story through letters is a technique known as **epistolary** form. Using letters to tell parts of the story makes the narrative appear more realistic.

Tension

Stevenson maintains a sense of tension and mystery throughout the novella which is only relieved in the final chapter. Keeping the reader in suspense is typical of both Gothic fiction and detective stories. Stevenson creates tension by:

- introducing mysterious questions.
- withholding information that could help to answer the mysterious questions.
- creating an uneasy mood through descriptions of characters, settings and events.
- ending chapters with cliff-hangers (see examples on **pages 14**, **16** and **17**).

Stevenson creates suspense for the reader.

Introducing questions

Most chapters in the novella introduce a mystery. For example:

Chapter One: Who is Mr Hyde?

Chapters Two and Three: Why does Mr Hyde have control over Jekyll?

Chapters Three and Six: Why have Jekyll and Lanyon fallen out?

Chapter Six: What happened to Lanyon to make him almost die from shock?

Chapter Seven: Why does Jekyll suddenly disappear from the window?

Chapter Eight: Who is locked in Jekyll's room?

Comment: These unanswered questions build the tension, and eventually lead Utterson to break down the door of Jekyll's cabinet (small room) with an axe.

Withholding information

Stevenson's characters often withhold information, or use vague and ambiguous language. This makes Utterson (and the reader) curious and suspicious:

Chapter One: Enfield refuses to say who signed the cheque.

Chapter Two: Lanyon won't say why he has fallen out with Jekyll (beyond *"fanciful"* science).

Chapter Three: Jekyll won't admit how he's involved with Hyde.

Chapter Six: Lanyon won't elaborate on the shocking incident he witnessed, or why he has fallen out with Jekyll again. He gives Utterson a letter which Utterson cannot open until Jekyll dies.

Chapter Seven: Jekyll won't tell Utterson why he is keeping himself locked inside his laboratory.

LANGUAGE TECHNIQUES

Stevenson uses lots of linguistic techniques in *Dr Jekyll and Mr Hyde*. You need to analyse techniques and be able to explain their impact on you as the reader to get good marks for AO2.

 It's not enough to just spot techniques. You also need to explain what effect these techniques have on you as the reader.

19th-century writing style

"Much of his past was unearthed, indeed, and all disreputable: tales came out of the man's cruelty, at once so callous and violent; of his vile life, of his strange associates, of the hatred that seemed to have surrounded his career; but of his present whereabouts, not a whisper."

Comment: Stevenson often uses long sentences punctuated with colons and semi-colons, as well as a formal writing style. This was typical of fiction writing in the 19th century.

Character-specific language

Stevenson creates distinct voices for each of the main characters which reinforces their personalities.

Mr Utterson's dialogue reinforces his rational nature.

Utterson — "If you have been inexact in any point you had better correct it."

Comment: To emphasise Utterson's character as a lawyer who tends to think and behave rationally, Stevenson uses precise, logical language.

Lanyon — "... seemed to contain phosphorus and some volatile ether."

Comment: In *Dr Lanyon's Narrative*, Lanyon uses technical language to describe some of the components he collects from Jekyll's laboratory. This reinforces Lanyon's character as an educated man of science.

When Lanyon watches Hyde transform into Jekyll, Stevenson makes Lanyon's language less controlled and more emotional. This emphasises the shock and disgust Lanyon feels.

Jekyll — "... in the agonised womb of consciousness, these polar twins should be struggling."

Comment: Jekyll's language in Chapter Ten is full of imagery. This contrasts with Utterson's precision and Lanyon's scientific language, suggesting that Jekyll is more creative and free-thinking.

Language techniques

Exclamations

Exclamations are sentences which end with an exclamation mark, and are used to show strong emotion, such as delight, surprise or fear.

> *"'O God!' I screamed, and "O God!" again and again"*

Stevenson uses exclamation marks in Lanyon's dialogue to show how disturbed he is by Jekyll's transformation.

Rhetorical questions

Rhetorical questions are questions that don't require an answer.

> *"If his messenger could go to one place, why could he not go to another?"*

Lanyon's rhetorical questions in his letter show his confusion at Jekyll's request.

Symbolism

Symbolism describes when an author uses a symbol to represent an idea.

Stevenson uses Jekyll's house to symbolise Jekyll's dual nature. The front of the house is respectable, with a *"great air of wealth and comfort"*. However, Jekyll's laboratory, which is connected to the rear of the house, is described as a *"sinister block of building"*. This shows how the house is both respectable and sinister, just like Jekyll.

Comment: There are other examples of symbolism. For example, fog reoccurs throughout the novella. This symbolises how some of the characters struggle to see what is in front of them: Jekyll's true nature.

Sensory language

Sensory language refers to words which relate to the five senses: sight, touch, smell, taste and sound.

> *"the bones were audibly shattered and the body jumped upon the roadway."*

Stevenson uses vivid language to describe the murder of Sir Danvers Carew. He describes the sound of Carew's bones breaking and how his body jumps as Hyde beats it. This emphasises the brutality of the attack, which shocks the reader.

Language techniques continued

Alliteration

Alliteration is when words which start with the same sound are grouped closely together in a sentence. This can be used to make a phrase or sentence more memorable.

| "... **d**ispleasing, something **d**own-right **d**etestable" | Enfield repeats words beginning with a 'd' sound when describing Hyde. This focuses the reader's attention on his description, which reinforces its significance. |

Personification

Personification is when something non-human is described as having human characteristics.

| "a pale moon, lying on her back as though the wind had tilted her" | Personifying the moon suggests that the wind is so strong it has caused the moon to fall over. |

Pathetic fallacy is similar to personification. It describes when something non-human displays emotion. For example, fog *"rolled over"* London after Carew's murder, as if it were concealing Hyde.

Semantic field

A **semantic field** is a group of words which are connected by meaning.

| "...snarled aloud into a savage laugh" | Hyde is often described using words from the semantic field of animals, such as *"snarled"*. This reinforces his primitive, sub-human nature, and contrasts with Utterson, who is described as *"eminently human"*. |

Similes

Similes describe something 'like' or 'as' something else.

| Soho (where Hyde lives) is described *"like a district of some city in a nightmare"*. | This gives the impression that Soho is a horrifying place, and further reinforces Hyde as a frightening and dreadful character. |

Metaphors

Metaphors describe something as being something else.

| "my blood was changed into something exquisitely thin and icy" | Jekyll describes how the blood ran cold in his veins when he turns into Hyde without drinking the potion. This describes the shock and terror he feels in this moment. |

CHAPTER ONE: STORY OF THE DOOR

Chapter One establishes the characters of Mr Utterson and the mysterious and wicked Mr Hyde.

Story of the Door

The reader is introduced to Mr Utterson, a lawyer. He's described as *"dusty, dreary and yet somehow lovable"* with an *"eminently human"* look in his eye.

Comment: Most of the story is told from the perspective of Utterson. It's important that he's established as a credible narrator, so the reader trusts his version of events. For more on the character of Utterson, turn to **page 32**.

He is presented as a patient and sympathetic man who has *"an approved tolerance for others"*.

Comment: Victorian society placed a lot of importance on reputation and behaving in a socially acceptable way. Utterson is described as *"the last good influence in the lives of downgoing men"*: he tries to be supportive of those who have been shunned by society. This helps to explain why he stands by Jekyll later in the novella. For more on reputation, turn to **page 42**.

Utterson goes for a walk around London every Sunday with his distant relative, Mr Enfield. Their walks look *"singularly dull"* to passers-by, but the men considered their Sunday walks *"the chief jewel of each week"*.

> Gentlemen were often expected to go for a stroll in public. They would dress smartly and greet other gentlemen to remind others of their place in society.

The men walk down a pleasant street with *"freshly painted shutters... and general cleanliness"* but notice a *"sinister"* building, showing *"sordid negligence"*.

Comment: Juxtaposing (deliberately placing two things next to each other) the description of the attractive buildings with the neglected building makes it seem even more unpleasant. The street also symbolises the theme of dual nature: it has both respectable and disreputable buildings on it. For more on this theme, **page 38**.

Enfield meets Hyde late one evening.

Enfield tells Utterson how he was walking past the neglected building once early in the morning, and he saw a man who bumped into a young girl, knocked her down and then *"trampled calmly"* over the child and left her *"screaming"*.

Comment: This is the reader's first introduction to Hyde, and this unprovoked and brutal attack immediately shapes their dislike of him.

Chapter One: Story of the Door continued

Enfield comments that the incident was *"hellish"*.

> **Comment:** Describing this unpleasant incident so early in the opening chapter sets the unsettling tone for the rest of the novella. The word *"hellish"* also links Hyde to the Devil. For more on the theme of religion, turn to **page 46**.

Enfield describes how a crowd gathered at the scene, and that he caught Hyde, who *"was perfectly cool and made no resistance"*.

> **Comment:** Hyde's lack of emotion shows how little he cares about what he has just done, presenting him as callous and remorseless. For more on Hyde, turn to **page 29**.

Although the girl isn't seriously hurt, Utterson threatens to ruin Hyde's reputation and *"make his name stink from one end of London to the other"*.

> **Comment:** This reinforces the importance of reputation in Victorian London. See **page 42**, for more on gentlemen and reputation.

Hyde agrees to pay the girl's family £100 in compensation, and he enters the neglected building with a key, and returns with a signed cheque.

> £100 in Victorian England would be worth about £8,000 today. This shows how much Hyde is prepared to pay to avoid a scandal.

Enfield says that the cheque was signed by *"a name that I can't mention… but it was a name at least very well known"* who is *"the very pink of the proprieties"* (the very definition of respectable). Enfield believes that Hyde is blackmailing whoever signed the cheque.

> **Comment:** Enfield tries to be discreet about the person who signed the cheque, but this increases the suspense: the reader wants to find out who he is, and how he's involved with Hyde. For more examples of how Stevenson creates tension, turn to **page 7**.

Enfield describes Hyde's appearance as *"down-right detestable"*.

> **Comment:** Throughout the novella, every character who meets Hyde describes how unpleasant he is and how uneasy he makes them feel. This establishes Hyde as a deeply unlikable character.

Utterson tells Enfield that he knows who signed the cheque, because he knows who lives in the building that Hyde entered. Enfield is ashamed of his *"long tongue"* (gossiping nature) and the two men agree never to mention the story again.

> **Comment:** Enfield believes he has acted in an ungentlemanly way by gossiping. This reinforces how gentleman were supposed to act with discretion.

CHAPTER TWO: SEARCH FOR MR HYDE

Utterson becomes suspicious of Mr Hyde, and is determined to meet him.

Search for Mr Hyde

That evening, at his home, Utterson goes to his safe to look at his friend, Dr Jekyll's, will.

Comment: Utterson is a lawyer, so he was responsible for drawing up Dr Jekyll's will: a legal document which outlines what should happen to Jekyll's belongings after he dies.

Utterson reads the will. It instructs that all Jekyll's belongings should be given to his *"friend and benefactor Edward Hyde"*. It also states that if Jekyll has an *"unexplained absence"*, that Mr Hyde should receive all of Dr Jekyll's possessions. Utterson thinks the will is an *"eyesore"* and he regrets drawing up the document.

Comment: Utterson is concerned by the will because he is a close friend of Jekyll, and he has never heard of Hyde. Utterson suspects that Jekyll was the man who signed the cheque, and that he is being blackmailed by Hyde.

Utterson goes to visit his friend, Dr Lanyon, who also knows Jekyll.

Lanyon tells Utterson that he doesn't see Jekyll anymore because *"he began to go wrong, wrong in the mind"*. Lanyon doesn't clarify exactly why he's no longer friends with Jekyll, but accuses Jekyll of *"unscientific balderdash"*, suggesting that Jekyll has been conducting experiments that Lanyon doesn't approve of.

Comment: When the novella was written, the scientific community disagreed over Darwin's Theory of Evolution (see **page 5**), so Utterson isn't especially concerned by Jekyll and Lanyon's falling out. However, this is ironic because Jekyll's scientific experiments are responsible for all the terrible things that happen in the novella. For more on the theme of science, see **page 46**.

Utterson asks Lanyon if he has ever heard of Hyde, and Lanyon replies *"never heard of him"*.

Comment: This deepens the mystery, as Utterson still doesn't know who Hyde is and how he's connected to Jekyll.

As he leaves Lanyon's house, Utterson still believes that Hyde is blackmailing Jekyll. Utterson comments that Jekyll was *"wild when he was young"* and thinks that Hyde is blackmailing Jekyll over *"the ghost of some old sin"*.

Comment: The description of Jekyll as being *"wild"* contradicts with an earlier description of him being *"the very pink of the proprieties"*. This hints that Jekyll has two sides to him. For more on the theme of dual nature, turn to **page 38**.

GCSE English Literature | Dr Jekyll and Mr Hyde

Chapter Two: Search for Mr Hyde continued

Utterson decides to keep watch of the neglected building that Hyde entered, to try to see Hyde for himself. After several days, Hyde finally appears.

Comment: When Utterson approaches Hyde, Hyde takes a *"hissing intake of breath"*. The word *"hissing"* makes Hyde sound sub-human.

Utterson introduces himself to Hyde, who is immediately defensive, and wants to know how Utterson knows his name. Utterson tells Hyde that they have *"common friends"*, including Jekyll. Mentioning Jekyll makes Hyde *"flush"* with anger, and he tells Utterson *"He never told you"*. Hyde *"snarled aloud into a savage laugh"* and then disappears inside the house.

Utterson confronts Hyde.

Comment: Utterson's first interaction with Hyde is tense and mysterious, and the reader is unsettled by Hyde.

Hyde is *"hardly human"* and makes Utterson feel *"disgust, loathing and fear"*.

Comment: Since the reader trusts Utterson, we believe and share his reaction to Hyde.

Utterson goes round the corner to a *"square of ancient, handsome houses"* and knocks on the door of a house which has a *"great air of wealth and comfort"*. This house belongs to Jekyll. Dr Jekyll's servant, Poole, answers the door and tells Utterson that Jekyll isn't at home.

Comment: This increases the tension. The audience suspect that Jekyll is somehow mixed up with Hyde, but they are still yet to meet him.

Utterson asks Poole about Hyde, and Poole admits that the servants *"have all orders to obey him"*, but that they *"see very little of him on this side of the house; he mostly comes and goes by the laboratory"*.

Comment: It's revealed that the neglected building that Hyde comes in and out of is Jekyll's laboratory, which is attached to the rear of Jekyll's house. The front of the house symbolises Jekyll's respectability, while the laboratory, which is connected to Hyde, symbolises a darker, more sinister side. For more on the theme of duality, turn to **page 38**.

Utterson leaves, and concludes that Jekyll is in *"deep waters"* because Hyde is blackmailing him. Utterson fears that Hyde may *"grow impatient to inherit"* and may try to kill Jekyll.

Comment: The end of this chapter ends with a cliff-hanger which creates suspense. The reader fears that Jekyll is in danger, and wonders whether Utterson will uncover the blackmail and save his friend before it is too late.

CHAPTER THREE: DR JEKYLL WAS QUITE AT EASE

Chapter Three is very short. The reader finally meets Dr Jekyll.

Dr Jekyll was Quite at Ease

Two weeks later, Jekyll invites Utterson over for dinner.

Comment: This is the first time the reader meets Jekyll. He is described as *"sincere"* and showing *"kindness"*, but he also has a *"slyish"* look about him, hinting that he can be deceptive.

This description suggests that Jekyll has both a good and a bad side to him: this duality is a reoccurring theme throughout the novella. For more on the character of Jekyll, turn to **page 27**.

Dr Jekyll is reluctant to speak about Hyde.

Utterson tells Jekyll that he disapproves of Jekyll's will, and that he has *"been learning something about young Hyde."* At the mention of Hyde, Jekyll *"grew pale"* and there was a *"blackness"* about his eyes.

Comment: It's clear from Jekyll's physical reaction that Hyde makes Jekyll uncomfortable, but Jekyll doesn't reveal why he feels uneasy.

Utterson is concerned about Jekyll, and offers to help him with Hyde.

Comment: This shows Utterson's compassionate nature. He is prepared to stand by Jekyll even if he is involved in something scandalous.

Jekyll refuses to give any details about Hyde, telling Utterson that the situation *"cannot be mended by talking"*.

Comment: Jekyll's language is very ambiguous. He says that he is *"painfully situated"* and that his position is *"strange"*, but he won't elaborate further. This increases the tension: Jekyll doesn't deny being involved with Hyde, but he won't talk about it with his close friend either.

Jekyll tries to reassure Utterson that he *"can be rid of Mr Hyde"* any time he wants, but Jekyll is unwilling to discuss Hyde anymore.

Comment: Utterson doesn't press Jekyll for more information. Utterson's gentlemanly behaviour prevents him from getting to the bottom of Jekyll and Hyde's relationship.

Jekyll makes Utterson promise to help Hyde when Jekyll is *"no longer here"*.

Comment: This conversion increases the mystery. Jekyll is reluctant to discuss Hyde, so it's not clear how the two men are connected. Jekyll seems afraid of Hyde, but he also wants Hyde to be taken care of if he dies. Mentioning death also creates an ominous atmosphere.

CHAPTER FOUR:
THE CAREW MURDER CASE

Hyde murders Sir Danvers Carew and he becomes a wanted man.

The Carew Murder Case

The story picks up almost a year later, describing a *"crime of singular ferocity"*. The crime is told from the perspective of a maid, who looks out of her bedroom window late one evening.

Comment: The night of the murder a fog *"rolled over the city"*. This image creates a sinister atmosphere, suggesting that an evil presence is spreading across London. Foggy weather is also a recurring feature of Gothic fiction, see **page 3**.

Hyde beats Danvers Carew to death.

She notices a *"gentleman with white hair"* talking with Hyde in the street below.

Comment: Light is often used to symbolise goodness, so when the moonlight shines on the gentleman's face, this implies he is an honourable character.

Suddenly, Hyde clubs the man with a cane in a fit of *"ape-like fury"*, shattering his bones.

Comment: The attack seems to be completely unprovoked: the victim *"bowed"* to Hyde and acted with *"politeness"*. The unnecessary violence towards an elderly man is horrifying.

The maid faints, wakes up hours later and calls the police. The victim lies *"mangled"* on the road, next to half of the cane which had broken because of the *"insensate cruelty"*.

A letter addressed to Mr Utterson was found on the body, so the police ask Utterson to come to the police station to help identify the victim. Utterson confirms that the man is Sir Danvers Carew.

Utterson recognises the cane as belonging to Jekyll, and Utterson and a police officer go to Hyde's house, but he isn't at home.

Comment: Hyde lives in Soho, an area in London that was associated with criminal behaviour in the 19th century. Stevenson describes Soho as *"a district of some city in a nightmare"*. This simile further links Hyde to immorality and evil.

Hyde's maid says that until last night, she hadn't seen Hyde for two months. Utterson and the officer search Hyde's house. The house was *"furnished with luxury and good taste"*, but had been *"recently and hurriedly ransacked"*. They find the other half of the cane that had been used to murder Sir Danvers Carew.

Comment: This chapter ends with another cliff-hanger. The reader knows that Hyde is responsible for the murder, but he has escaped the police and is still at large. This makes the reader wonder if he will kill again.

CHAPTER FIVE: INCIDENT OF THE LETTER

Utterson visits Jekyll at his laboratory. Jekyll has received a letter from Hyde confirming that he is on the run following the murder of Sir Danvers Carew.

Incident of the Letter

Utterson visits Jekyll and is escorted to Jekyll's laboratory. It is the first time Utterson has been inside the laboratory, which is described as *"dingy, windowless"*.

Comment: The laboratory used to be *"dissecting rooms"* (rooms used to cut open dead bodies). This association with death adds to the unpleasant nature of laboratory.

Jekyll looks *"deathly sick"* and speaks in a *"changed voice"*. Jekyll tells Utterson that Hyde will *"never more be heard of"*.

Utterson visits Jekyll in his laboratory.

Comment: Jekyll doesn't reveal why he is unwell nor why Hyde won't be heard from again. This adds to the mystery.

Jekyll shows Utterson a letter written by Hyde which was hand-delivered that day. The letter reveals that Hyde has run away.

Comment: Gothic fiction often uses letters to reveal plot points (see **page 3** for more).

Jekyll reveals that Hyde *"dictated the terms"* in Jekyll's will. Utterson takes this as proof that Hyde intended to murder Jekyll.

As he leaves Jekyll's house, Utterson asks Poole whether he saw whoever delivered Hyde's letter. Poole tells him that no letters had been delivered that day.

Comment: Utterson believes that the letter must have been hand-delivered to Jekyll by someone at the laboratory door, or it was written by Hyde inside the laboratory.

Later that day, Utterson discusses Hyde's letter with his head clerk, Mr Guest. Mr Guest looks at the handwriting and suggests that it is very similar to Dr Jekyll's.

Comment: Utterson asks Mr Guest not to *"speak of this note"*. He wants to keep it a secret to protect Jekyll's reputation.

Utterson believes that Jekyll has forged the note for Hyde, and his *"blood ran cold in his veins"*.

Comment: Utterson is horrified that Jekyll is still covering for Hyde, even after the murder. This chapter ends with another cliff-hanger, increasing the tension for the reader.

CHAPTER SIX: INCIDENT OF DR LANYON

Utterson visits Lanyon, who appears to be close to death.

Incident of Dr Lanyon

For two months, Jekyll appears to have a new lease of life. He *"did good"* and his *"face seemed to open and brighten"*. Jekyll repairs his relationship with Dr Lanyon.

Suddenly, Jekyll shuts himself away again, and refuses to see anyone.

Utterson visits Dr Lanyon, but he is alarmed by Lanyon's appearance: *"his death-warrant written legibly on his face"* with a look of *"deep-seated terror"*. Lanyon confirms that he has had a *"shock"* that has brought him close to death.

Comment: Lanyon doesn't reveal what this shock was until Chapter Nine. This heightens the suspense for the reader as they wonder what has happened to him.

Utterson asks Dr Lanyon about Jekyll, and Lanyon replies: *"I am quite done with that person"*. He also regards Jekyll as *"dead"*.

Comment: This increases the mystery. Lanyon refuses to explain why his relationship with Jekyll has been destroyed.

Unable to see Jekyll in-person, Utterson writes to Jekyll asking why he will no longer see him.

Jekyll sends a reply and tells Utterson that he intends to lead a life of *"extreme seclusion"* because he is *"the chief of sinners"*.

Comment: Jekyll hints that he has done something wicked, but he won't elaborate or ask Utterson for help. Jekyll's secretive nature is one of the driving forces of the novella. For more on the theme of secrecy, turn to **page 50**.

A few weeks later, Dr Lanyon dies. Lanyon leaves Utterson a letter that is *"not to be opened till the death or disappearance of Dr. Henry Jekyll"*.

Utterson, compelled by his *"professional honour"*, locks the letter in his safe without reading the contents.

Comment: Utterson's decision to not read the letter shows his integrity. Although the letter will probably help explain why Jekyll is behaving so strangely, Utterson respects Lanyon's wishes and doesn't read it.

CHAPTER SEVEN: INCIDENT AT THE WINDOW

Utterson and Enfield see Jekyll at his laboratory window, but the encounter is interrupted by Jekyll's sudden disappearance.

Incident at the Window

Utterson and Enfield are enjoying their regular Sunday walk.

Comment: This chapter starts in a similar way to Chapter One with Utterson and Enfield walking past the sinister door where Enfield told the story of Hyde trampling the young girl. This may set the reader on edge, as they may anticipate that something dramatic will happen here again.

They pass the street near Jekyll's laboratory. It is *"cool and a little damp and full of premature twilight"* even though the rest of the sky was still *"bright with sunset"*.

Comment: This description implies that Jekyll's laboratory emits a gloomy and cold atmosphere, even though the surrounding area is *"bright"*. This reinforces Jekyll's laboratory as something unpleasant and sinister.

They look up at a window and see Jekyll.

Utterson asks Jekyll if he is feeling better, to which Jekyll responds that he is feeling *"very low"* and declines to leave the laboratory to walk with Utterson and Enfield.

Suddenly, a look of *"abject terror and despair"* crosses Jekyll's face, and he shuts the window and disappears.

Something shocks Jekyll while he is at his window.

Comment: Stevenson doesn't give much detail about what happens or what Enfield and Utterson witness. This leaves the reader to wonder what they have seen.

The incident *"froze the very blood"* of Enfield and Utterson, and Utterson exclaims: *"God forgive us"*.

Comment: Utterson asking God for forgiveness implies that he has witnessed something unholy or unnatural.

CHAPTER EIGHT: THE LAST NIGHT

This is the last chapter told from the perspective of Utterson. Poole asks Utterson to come to Jekyll's house because he's worried about his master.

The Last Night

Utterson is at home when he receives a visit from Poole who tells him that there is *"something wrong"* with Jekyll and he can *"bear it no more"*. Poole is reluctant to tell Utterson what has happened and asks that Utterson come to Jekyll's house to see for himself.

Comment: As the men travel to Jekyll's house, Stevenson describes the weather as *"wild"* and how the wind *"flecked the blood into the face"*. Although this means that the wind made the men's faces red, it conjures a terrifying image of blood-spattered faces.

When Poole and Utterson arrive at Jekyll's house, the rest of the household staff are *"huddled together like a flock of sheep"*, *"hysterical"*.

Comment: Utterson comments that the servants' behaviour is *"Very irregular, very unseemly"*. This emphasises how frightened the servants are: they are unable to control themselves and act in the proper way.

Poole leads Utterson across the courtyard to the laboratory, and warns Utterson: *"I don't want you to be heard… if by any chance he was to ask you in, don't go."*

Comment: Poole's warning to Utterson makes the reader feel uneasy. It suggests that Jekyll could be capable of violence and that Utterson might be in danger.

Poole speaks to Jekyll from outside the cabinet door. Poole leads Utterson back into the house, and asks: *"Was that my master's voice?"* Utterson admits that the voice seems *"much changed"*.

A 'cabinet' was a 'small, private room'.

Poole confesses that Jekyll has been locked away for eight days *"crying night and day for some sort of medicine"*. Jekyll had given the servants a note to take to the chemists to try to find a chemical that he needed, but what they return with is *"impure"* and *"useless"*.

Comment: Poole's description of Jekyll's odd behaviour builds a sense of foreboding in the reader: they suspect that something is terribly wrong.

Poole recalls that he interrupted Jekyll one day *"digging through the crates"* in the laboratory. When he noticed Poole, Jekyll appeared to be wearing a *"mask"* and cried *"like a rat"* and ran back into his room.

Comment: Comparing Jekyll to a rat reminds the audience of the animalistic language used to describe Hyde.

Chapter Eight: The Last Night continued

Utterson suggests that Jekyll has a mysterious illness which would explain his altered voice, reluctance to see friends and his desperation to find a drug to cure him.

Comment: This emphasises Utterson's rational outlook. He wants to find a logical explanation for Jekyll's strange behaviour.

Poole tells Utterson that Jekyll was a *"tall, fine build of a man"* but the man he caught in the laboratory was *"more of a dwarf"*. Poole insists that the *"thing in the mask was never Dr Jekyll"*.

Comment: This description would remind the reader of Hyde.

The men agree to break down the door to Jekyll's cabinet to see who is inside. Before they attempt to break down the door, Utterson says *"We both think more than we have said"*.

Comment: Utterson acknowledges that both he and Poole know more than they have admitted. This shows how Victorian gentlemen would prefer to avoid saying something scandalous, even in a life and death situation.

Poole admits that the *"masked thing like a monkey"* he saw in Jekyll's laboratory was almost certainly Hyde.

Utterson believes that Jekyll has been murdered by Hyde and that Hyde is locked in Jekyll's study. As they prepare to break down the door, Utterson calls out: *"Jekyll… I demand to see you"*. A voice inside the laboratory calls back *"have mercy!"* and Utterson recognises it as Hyde's voice. They break down the door to the cabinet with an axe.

Comment: The door symbolises Jekyll's secrecy: when the door is broken, Jekyll's secrets are finally revealed. For more on the theme of secrecy, turn to **page 50**.

When they enter the room, they find the body of Hyde *"contorting and still twitching"*. He has killed himself by drinking poison. Utterson and Poole search the laboratory for Jekyll's body, but they cannot find him.

They notice a *"cheval-glass"* (full-length tilting mirror) which has been positioned horizontally so the mirror is facing the ceiling.

Comment: This suggests that whoever was in the cabinet didn't want to look at their reflection.

They also find a letter, addressed to Utterson. Inside is a new version of Jekyll's will which has been changed and now gives everything to Utterson. There is a note, which instructs Utterson to read the letter that Lanyon gave him, and a packet of sealed papers.

Utterson leaves Jekyll's house to go to read the letter that Lanyon gave him in Chapter Six.

GCSE English Literature | Dr Jekyll and Mr Hyde

CHAPTER NINE: DR LANYON'S NARRATIVE

Utterson finally reads the letter that Dr Lanyon gave him. This letter helps to explain some of Jekyll's mysterious behaviour.

Dr Lanyon's Narrative

This chapter is presented as a narrative written by Lanyon.

Comment: Revealing information through letters is typical of the Gothic fiction genre. It also allows the reader to experience a shift in perspective, and see events from a different character's point of view, allowing gaps in the narrative to be filled in. Lanyon's letter provides a flashback to early January, just as Jekyll began to isolate himself from his friends.

Lanyon describes how he receives a letter from Jekyll. The letter instructs Lanyon to go to Jekyll's house, and take a drawer from his laboratory which contains *"some powders, a phial* [small bottle] *and a paper book"*, and then to be alone in his consulting room at midnight and to allow a man with Jekyll's name to enter.

Comment: Stevenson uses several rhetorical questions in this part of Lanyon's narrative to express his confusion and disbelief at the request.

Lanyon follows the instructions and goes to Jekyll's lab to retrieve the drawer. The phial holds a *"blood-red"* liquid, and the book contains a record of some experiments that Jekyll had been conducting.

Comment: Comparing the colour of the liquid to blood creates an ominous atmosphere.

Afraid, Lanyon waits for the man to arrive, but he *"loaded an old revolver"* to protect himself.

Comment: This increases the suspense. Lanyon arms himself because he's worried he might be in danger.

At midnight, the man arrives at Lanyon's house.

Comment: Hyde often operates at night (for example when he stamps on the young girl and when he murders Sir Danvers Carew). This links Hyde with both literal and figurative darkness.

Instantly Lanyon is uneasy and feels a *"disturbance"* and *"disgustful curiosity"* by his presence.

Comment: The reader recognises that the stranger is Hyde. This creates dramatic irony and heightens the tension. The reader knows that Hyde is capable of terrible violence, and they wonder what his business is with Dr Lanyon.

Chapter Nine: Dr Lanyon's Narrative continued

The man is desperate to see the contents of the drawer, and is in a state of near *"hysteria"*. When Lanyon points out the drawer, the man gives a sigh of *"immense relief"* and begins to mix a concoction.

When he has made the concoction, the man asks Lanyon whether the *"greed of curiosity"* has overwhelmed him, and if Lanyon wants the man to drink the mixture in front of him.

> **Comment:** This moment has similarities between the story of Adam and Eve in the Bible. Satan tempts Eve to eat from the tree of knowledge, which causes Adam and Eve to be expelled from the garden of Eden. Here, Hyde tempts Lanyon's curiosity with a sight that will *"stagger the unbelief of Satan"*. The consequence of Lanyon's curiosity is his eventual death from shock.

Hyde drinks a potion to turn into Jekyll.

Lanyon agrees to watch him drink the potion. As he drinks, the man turns into Jekyll.

> **Comment:** Although many readers may already know (or may have guessed) the twist, this is the first time that Stevenson confirms that Jekyll and Hyde are the same person.

The description of the man's transformation into Jekyll is visceral. He is described as *"gasping with open mouth"* and he seems to *"swell"* and his features *"melt and alter"*.

> **Comment:** The transformation takes its toll on Jekyll, who is described as looking like a man *"restored from death"*. This sinister description reinforces the idea that the science that Jekyll uses to transform himself is not natural.

Lanyon admits that he has been deeply affected by what he has witnessed: *"My life is shaken to its roots; sleep has left me; the deadliest terror sits by me at all hours of the day"*.

> **Comment:** Lanyon's reaction suggests that he isn't amazed or impressed by what he has witnessed. Instead, he's appalled and views it as something unnatural and evil. The shock is so overwhelming that it eventually kills him.

Lanyon admits that the man who drank the mixture in front of him was Hyde.

> **Comment:** When he sees Jekyll, Lanyon screams *""O God!" again and again"*. Lanyon's hysterical reaction contrasts with his previous characterisation as a rational man of science. Victorian gentlemen were expected to stay in control of their emotions, so Lanyon's outburst shows how deeply the shock has affected him.

CHAPTER TEN: HENRY JEKYLL'S FULL STATEMENT OF THE CASE

The final chapter is told via a letter written by Jekyll. It explains exactly what happened and why.

Henry Jekyll's Full Statement of the Case

Comment: Jekyll's letter allows the reader to understand his motivation for creating Hyde, and answers any remaining questions that readers might have.

Jekyll explains that he was born to a wealthy family and was encouraged to work hard to make sure he had *"an honourable and distinguished future"*. From a young age, Jekyll found it difficult to reconcile how he should act in public, with how he felt inside. He admits to hiding his *"pleasures"* with a *"morbid sense of shame"*.

Comment: This suggests that Jekyll was under a lot of pressure to behave in a certain way and felt guilt at even the slightest wrongdoing. Many Victorian readers may have empathised with Jekyll and his experiences of a repressive and judgemental society.

He began to develop a dual nature of *"good and evil"* and admits that both sides of his personality were equal. He was truly himself when he *"plunged into shame"* as well as when he *"laboured… at the furtherance of knowledge"*.

Comment: Dual nature is an important theme in the novella. Turn to **page 38** for more.

Jekyll pursued science that was *"mystic"* and *"transcendental"*, and he focused on a *"beloved daydream"* to split himself into two individuals, so that the *"unjust"* side of him could be free from *"remorse"* and the *"just"* side could be protected from *"evil"*.

Jekyll created a potion which he hoped would split his identity, but drinking it might *"risk death"*.

Comment: This shows how determined Jekyll was to separate the two sides of his personality. He was prepared to drink the potion, even though it might kill him.

When he drinks the potion and becomes Hyde for the first time, he feels *"younger, lighter, happier"* but also *"tenfold more wicked"*.

Comment: Without Jekyll's good side to balance him out, Hyde is completely evil.

Jekyll explains that Hyde's appearance is also influenced by his evil nature, which left *"an imprint of deformity and decay"*.

Comment: Some Victorians believed in **physiognomy**: the idea that a person's facial features could tell you about their character. Stevenson's descriptions of Hyde's unpleasant appearance would have reinforced the idea that he was evil and wicked.

Henry Jekyll's Full Statement of the Case continued

He drinks the potion again, and he transforms back into Jekyll.

> **Comment:** Jekyll comments that the potion only causes him to split into the evil Hyde. When he becomes Jekyll again, he's a mixture of both good and evil. The discovery of the potion moves him *"wholly towards the worse"*. This emphasises how Jekyll was motivated to create the potion so he could behave immorally, rather than creating a version of himself that was entirely good.

Jekyll is initially hesitant to drink the potion.

Jekyll describes how he makes changes in his life to accommodate Hyde. He sets up a house for him in Soho, and hires an *"unscrupulous maid"*. He tells his servants to give Hyde *"full liberty"* and drew up the will.

> **Comment:** These preparations suggest that Hyde will be a permanent fixture in Jekyll's life. Jekyll wants to be able to transform into Hyde whenever he wants.

Jekyll admits that prior to creating Hyde, he would sometime indulge in *"undignified"* behaviour, but when he was Hyde, his behaviour would be *"monstrous"*.

> **Comment:** This creates some sympathy for Jekyll. He never intended to do truly evil things, he just wanted to have some freedom from the burden of respectability. Jekyll was sometimes *"aghast"* at Hyde's actions and would try to *"undo the evil done by Hyde"*.

Jekyll doesn't give details about Hyde's *"infamy"*.

> **Comment:** Not elaborating on the details of his evil actions means that it is up to the reader to imagine what Hyde did. This involves the reader and forces them to draw inspiration from their own misdeeds.

Two months before the Danvers Carew murder, Jekyll describes how he had gone to sleep as Jekyll, but he had woken up as Hyde without taking the potion. He notices that Hyde had grown taller, and Jekyll worried that his nature *"might be permanently overthrown"*.

> **Comment:** This implies that Hyde is growing stronger, and is starting to overwhelm Jekyll. Stevenson could be warning his readers of the consequences of indulging in destructive behaviour and how it can take control of your life.

Jekyll decides to stop taking the potion to turn into Hyde, but he doesn't give up Hyde's house in Soho or destroy Hyde's clothes.

> **Comment:** Even though Hyde is destroying him, Jekyll is unwilling to erase Hyde completely. This shows that evil still has a hold over Jekyll.

For two months, Jekyll doesn't turn into Hyde, but he is *"tortured with throes and longings"* to be Hyde again, and he eventually gives in to temptation and drinks the potion.

Chapter Ten: Henry Jekyll's Full Statement of the Case continued

After being repressed for so long, Hyde has a *"more furious propensity to ill"* when he is released, and when Hyde kills Sir Danvers Carew, the *"spirit of hell"* raged within him.

> **Comment:** Stevenson uses language to link Hyde to the Devil to show how evil he truly is.

After killing Carew, he transforms back into Jekyll, and is haunted by the *"hideous images and sounds"* of the murder. Jekyll once again pledges to not turn into Hyde.

Later, Jekyll spontaneously transforms into Hyde in public. Hyde knows he is wanted for Carew's murder, so he can't go to Jekyll's laboratory to get the potion to turn himself back into Jekyll.

> **Comment:** Hyde knows he would be sent *"to the gallows"* (hanged for the murder) if he was caught. Victorian England punished murderers with the death penalty.

Instead, he hides in a hotel, and writes the letter to Lanyon, asking him to go to the laboratory to fetch the potion.

> **Comment:** Jekyll doesn't give much detail about his incident with Lanyon. This prevents too much repetition with the previous chapter.

After his meeting with Lanyon, Jekyll returns home, but once again, he turns into Hyde without the potion. It took a *"double dose"* to transform back into Jekyll.

> **Comment:** Jekyll is turning into Hyde more easily, but finding it more difficult to switch back to Jekyll. This highlights the struggle between Jekyll's two natures, and how the evil is starting to overwhelm him.

As Hyde, he torments Jekyll by burning Jekyll's letters, and destroying a portrait of Jekyll's father.

> **Comment:** Hyde punishes Jekyll, even though they are two sides of the same person. This emphasises the internal conflict caused by Jekyll's dual nature.

The ingredients that Jekyll needs to create the potion have run out, and Jekyll knows that it won't be long before he loses control of Hyde forever.

> **Comment:** Some critics have suggested that the novella is a metaphor for drug addiction. Jekyll consumes a substance which changes his behaviour, and becomes addictive. Eventually, Jekyll must take more of the substance, just to feel like himself again. Drug use was on the rise in Victorian England, and drugs like cocaine and opium (a form of heroin) were frequently used in medicine, although few people were aware of the dangers of substance abuse.

The letter ends with Jekyll wondering whether Hyde will be hanged for the murder of Carew or whether he will decide to kill himself instead.

> **Comment:** The story ends without a reaction from Utterson or the other characters. This makes the ending feel sudden and jarring.

CHARACTERS: HENRY JEKYLL / EDWARD HYDE

Jekyll is a seemingly respectable doctor, but he's secretly conducting supernatural experiments. He wants to break free from the constraints of Victorian society without damaging his reputation.

Comment: Jekyll is the **protagonist**, but he only speaks directly in four of the ten chapters. The reader mainly learns about him through the opinions of other characters. It's only in the final chapter that Jekyll reveals all. This maintains a mystery around his character until the very end.

Mysterious: Before the reader meets Jekyll, he is presented as mysterious: the reader knows he's mixed up with Hyde in some way but it's not clear how the two are connected.

Jekyll is torn between his reputation and his desire to behave sinfully.

Comment: This creates anticipation. The reader knows Jekyll is a gentleman and a respectable doctor, but they also know that he is also involved with the evil, and disreputable Hyde.

Gentleman: Jekyll socialises with *"intelligent, reputable men"*. He is known for his *"charities"* and is a Christian.

Comment: Outwardly, Jekyll seems like perfect gentleman, but Stevenson uses the character of Jekyll to show how appearances can be deceptive.

Secretive: From a young age, Jekyll *"concealed his pleasures"* to protect his reputation. He creates Hyde so he can secretly do immoral things, and he doesn't tell anyone about Hyde until it's too late.

Comment: Jekyll's secretive nature is a reoccurring theme throughout the novel (see **page 50**), and his unwillingness to reveal his secrets force him into a destructive double-life that eventually leads to his downfall

Radical: Jekyll and Lanyon fall out over Jekyll's *"fanciful"* scientific experiments.

Comment: Jekyll is prepared to damage his friendships to pursue his science. He prioritises his *"beloved daydream"* of creating Hyde over almost everything else.

Desperate: Jekyll knows he *"risked death"* when he first drinks the potion to turn into Hyde. This shows how desperate he is: he'd rather risk death than continue to repress his evil side.

Comment: This is ironic. Although Jekyll doesn't die when he first drinks the potion, Hyde eventually kills Jekyll when he dies by suicide.

Henry Jekyll / Edward Hyde continued

Self-satisfied: At first, Jekyll finds his ability to transform into Hyde *"humorous"*. He likes having a secret second identity.

Comment: Initially, Jekyll can't see any downsides to Hyde. He believes he has created the ideal solution to protecting his reputation while also being able to do immoral things without feeling shame.

Weak: After Hyde's behaviour worsens, Jekyll pledges to stop turning into Hyde. However, Jekyll cannot resist temptation, and he turns into Hyde again.

Comment: Even though Jekyll is *"aghast"* at Hyde's behaviour and knows that he's putting people in danger when he turns into Hyde, Jekyll's desire to behave immorally is too powerful.

Jekyll is the only character who experiences *"no repugnance"* when he sees Hyde. This could be because Jekyll admires the evil inside himself.

Repressed: Jekyll admits he created Hyde to escape the *"unbearable"* pressure of trying to protect his reputation.

Comment: This may have created some sympathy with Victorian readers. Many people would have recognised the pressure from society to maintain a 'perfect' reputation.

The relationship between Jekyll and Hyde changes throughout the novella. At first, Jekyll is desperate to create Hyde so that he can indulge in misdeeds without damaging his reputation, and he's delighted with the freedom that Hyde gives him.

However, Hyde grows stronger and eventually starts to overpower Jekyll, as the two identities compete to take full control. Eventually, Jekyll *"hated and feared the thought of the brute"*.

! Note

Stevenson presents Jekyll as a typical Victorian gentleman who, like most people, is a mix of both good and bad. This makes Jekyll an identifiable character and hints that most people have a Hyde within them.

This would have been an uncomfortable realisation to many Victorian readers.

Remember that Jekyll and Hyde are the same person, even though Jekyll tries to distance himself from Hyde by giving him a different name and a separate place to live in Soho. Jekyll often refers to Hyde in the third person to disassociate himself from Hyde.

Jekyll grows weaker as Hyde grows stronger.

CHARACTERS: HENRY JEKYLL / EDWARD HYDE

Hyde is a repellent character who enjoys hurting those around him.

Henry Jekyll / Edward Hyde continued

The name 'Hyde' is pronounced like 'hide'. This reinforces how Hyde is hidden within Jekyll.

Hyde is completely evil.

Animalistic: Throughout the novella, Stevenson compares Hyde's appearance and behaviour to animals, such as *"ape-like fury"* and *"like a monkey"*.

Comment: He's also described as being short and *"hairy"*. This implies he is physically less evolved than the other characters, which would also remind readers of Darwin's Theory of Evolution (see **page 5**).

Disturbing: Everyone who meets Hyde is struck by a sense of unease and disgust.

Comment: As well as being repulsive, Hyde brings out the worst in people. The doctor who attends the trampled girl turned *"sick and white with the desire to kill him"*.

Evil: He tramples a young girl and he murders Sir Danvers Carew. Both acts of violence are unprovoked, and he shows no remorse. Hyde just wants to hurt people.

Comment: Because Hyde only represents Jekyll's evil side, there is no goodness in him to moderate his behaviour. Jekyll wanted to create Hyde so that he could do *"undignified"* things, but Hyde commits crimes far worse than Jekyll intended.

Tempting: Hyde asks Lanyon if he wants to watch him drink the potion, even though he suspects it will *"stagger the unbelief of Satan"* and change Lanyon for the worse.

Comment: In Christian teaching, the Devil tempts Adam and Eve in the garden of Eden to eat from the tree of knowledge. In the novella, Hyde tempts Lanyon to watch him transform because it will provide a *"new province of knowledge"*. Tempting mankind with knowledge links Hyde with Satan.

Powerful: Eventually, Hyde grows stronger and begins to take control of Jekyll without the potion. Hyde torments Jekyll by destroying his belongings.

Comment: Jekyll recognises that once the potion runs out, he will lose control of Hyde altogether. Stevenson could be suggesting that, if given the chance, the evil side of mankind will always overwhelm the good.

In this extract from the chapter entitled *Henry Jekyll's Full Statement of the Case*, Jekyll describes the murder of Sir Danvers Carew.

> *Instantly the spirit of hell awoke in me and raged. With a transport of glee, I mauled the unresisting body, tasting delight from every blow; and it was not till weariness had begun to succeed, that I was suddenly, in the top fit of my delirium, struck through the heart by a cold thrill of terror. A mist dispersed; I saw my life to be forfeit; and fled from the scene of these excesses, at once glorying and trembling, my lust of evil gratified and stimulated, my love of life screwed to the topmost peg. I ran to the house in Soho, and (to make assurance doubly sure) destroyed my papers; thence I set out through the lamplit streets, in the same divided ecstasy of mind, gloating on my crime, light-headedly devising others in the future, and yet still hastening and still hearkening in my wake for the steps of the avenger. Hyde had a song upon his lips as he compounded the draught, and as he drank it, pledged the dead man. The pangs of transformation had not done tearing him, before Henry Jekyll, with streaming tears of gratitude and remorse, had fallen upon his knees and lifted his clasped hands to God. The veil of self-indulgence was rent from head to foot. I saw my life as a whole: I followed it up from the days of childhood, when I had walked with my father's hand, and through the self-denying toils of my professional life, to arrive again and again, with the same sense of unreality, at the damned horrors of the evening. I could have screamed aloud; I sought with tears and prayers to smother down the crowd of hideous images and sounds with which my memory swarmed against me; and still, between the petitions, the ugly face of my iniquity stared into my soul. As the acuteness of this remorse began to die away, it was succeeded by a sense of joy. The problem of my conduct was solved. Hyde was thenceforth impossible; whether I would or not, I was now confined to the better part of my existence; and O, how I rejoiced to think of it! With what willing humility I embraced anew the restrictions of natural life! with what sincere renunciation I locked the door by which I had so often gone and come, and ground the key under my heel!*

Starting with this extract, explore how Stevenson presents ideas about good and evil in *Strange Case of Dr Jekyll and Mr Hyde*.

Write about:
- how Stevenson presents ideas about good and evil in this extract
- how Stevenson presents ideas about good and evil in the novella as a whole.

[30 marks]

Your answer may include:

AO1 — show understanding of the text
- *Hyde is presented as truly evil throughout the novella. In this extract, he experiences "delight" from beating Danvers Carew to death, and feels no guilt, shame or disgust.*
- *Stevenson juxtaposes Hyde's description of the crime with Jekyll's reaction. Since Jekyll has a good side to his character, he feels "remorse" and cries when he recalls the "hideous images and sounds" of the murder. However, Jekyll's guilt and sorrow doesn't last long. He "rejoiced" when he realises that if he doesn't transform into Hyde again, Hyde cannot be caught for the crime. This shows how Jekyll has an evil side too: he doesn't take responsibility for Hyde, and prioritises his reputation over justice for the murder.*
- *Elsewhere in the novel, Stevenson explores how the duality of being both good and bad weighs heavily on Jekyll, and this, along with the expectations of a repressive Victorian society, causes him to split his identity into two so he can commit misdeeds without damaging his reputation as a gentleman.*
- *The struggle between good and evil eventually causes tension between Jekyll and Hyde, as Hyde begins to overpower Jekyll by spontaneously appearing. This suggests that evil can completely overwhelm a person's character if allowed to do so.*

AO2 — show understanding of the writer's language choices
- *When talking about Hyde, Jekyll switches between the first person ("I saw my life to be forfeit") and third person ("Hyde had a song upon his lips"). This shows Jekyll's conflicted feelings towards Hyde: he tries to distance himself from Hyde, but also acknowledges that Hyde is a part of him.*
- *Stevenson uses vivid imagery to describe the evil nature of Hyde's crime. The verb "mauled" has associations of animals destroying their prey, and suggests that Hyde was in a frenzy.*
- *Sir Danvers Carew isn't dignified with a name, instead he is referred to as the "unresisting body" showing how Jekyll doesn't even acknowledge Carew's humanity.*

AO3 — relate the novella to the context
- *Stevenson presents Jekyll as mix of both good and evil, and this makes him identifiable to readers, suggesting that human nature is neither entirely good nor entirely bad. The character of Jekyll suggests that most people have a 'Hyde' trapped inside them, but Stevenson warns about the dangers of letting it free.*
- *Stevenson also could be criticising repressive Victorian society which encouraged people to lead completely spotless lives. Stevenson could be suggesting that these expectations can be damaging, as repressing "undignified" behaviour can lead people to do "monstrous" things.*

This answer should be marked in accordance with the levels-based mark scheme on page 53.

Make sure your answer to this question is in paragraphs and full sentences. Bullet points have been used in this example answer to suggest some information you could include.

CHARACTERS: GABRIEL UTTERSON

Mr Utterson is a lawyer and close friend to Dr Jekyll. He is honourable and sympathetic, and tries to help those in trouble.

Most of the novella is told from the perspective of Utterson, so it's important that Stevenson presents him as a likeable and reliable narrator so that the readers trust his account of events.

Utterson tries to find rational explanations for Jekyll's strange behaviour.

Serious: His face is *"never lighted by a smile"*, and he's described as *"dusty, dreary"*.

Comment: Utterson is presented as a serious man who doesn't show his emotions readily. Victorian men were expected to keep their emotions hidden. Although he seems to be very serious and unemotional, he cares deeply about his friends, particularly Jekyll, showing how outward appearances can be deceptive.

Sympathetic: Utterson *"inclined to help rather than to reprove"*. He tries to help people, rather than criticise them.

Comment: Unlike most of Victorian society at the time, Utterson is forgiving of peoples' mistakes, and tries not to judge. This explains why he's willing to help Jekyll, even though he suspects he could be involved in something scandalous.

Educated: Utterson is a lawyer who helped to draw up Jekyll's will.

Comment: Utterson's dialogue is often quite wordy. This reflects his profession as a lawyer.

Gentleman: Utterson conforms to expectations of Victorian gentlemen. He tries to be discreet (when Mr Guest recognises Jekyll's handwriting on the note from Hyde, he asks him not to speak of it again); reserved (he doesn't force Jekyll to tell him about his involvement with Hyde); and proper (he scolds Jekyll's servants for being *"unseemly"*).

Comment: Despite his gentlemanly nature, the expectations of behaving in a socially acceptable way cause Utterson to feel *"envy"* towards those people who commit misdeeds. This suggests that, like Jekyll, he sometimes craves the freedom to do whatever he wants.

Gabriel Utterson continued

Inquisitive: When Enfield first tells Utterson about Hyde, Utterson decides to investigate Hyde, and spends days watching the laboratory door.

> **Comment:** Utterson's curiosity goes against typical gentlemanly behaviour. This shows how concerned he is for Jekyll: he's prepared to act in a socially unacceptable way to help protect his friend.

Honourable: When Utterson receives a letter from Lanyon that could help explain what is happening, *"professional honour"* prevents him from opening it.

> **Comment:** Choosing not to read the letter is very in-keeping with Utterson's character, but it's also an important dramatic device which allows Stevenson to conceal the plot twist until the very end.

Utterson takes it upon himself to investigate Hyde.

Rational: Utterson tries to find logical, rational explanations for the strange events of the novella, even though this means he often jumps to the wrong conclusions. He initially thinks that Hyde is blackmailing Jekyll, and later believes Jekyll is suffering from a *"cerebral disease"*.

> **Comment:** Victorian readers of Gothic fiction would have suspected that there may be a supernatural explanation for Jekyll's odd behaviour. This creates dramatic irony, where the reader knows more than the characters.

Loyal: When Jekyll locks himself in his laboratory, Poole turns to Utterson for help. Poole knows that Utterson can be trusted, and won't turn his back on Jekyll in his hour of need.

> **Comment:** Utterson is prepared to put himself in danger by trying to apprehend a known murderer to help save Jekyll.

The reader never discovers Utterson's reaction to Lanyon and Jekyll's letters in the final chapters. Instead, the reader must come to their own conclusions about Jekyll's actions, without being influenced by Utterson's opinion.

GCSE English Literature | Dr Jekyll and Mr Hyde

In this extract from the chapter entitled *The Carew Murder Case*, Sir Danvers Carew has been murdered by Hyde, and Utterson and a police officer travel to Hyde's house in Soho to try to apprehend the murderer.

    It was by this time about nine in the morning, and the first fog of the season. A great chocolate-coloured pall* lowered over heaven, but the wind was continually charging and routing these embattled vapours; so that as the cab crawled from street to street, Mr. Utterson beheld a marvellous number of degrees and hues of twilight; for here it would be dark like the back-end of evening; and there would be a glow of a rich, lurid brown, like the light of some strange conflagration; and here, for a moment, the fog would be quite broken up, and a haggard shaft of daylight would glance in between the swirling wreaths. The dismal quarter of Soho seen under these changing glimpses, with its muddy ways, and slatternly passengers, and its lamps, which had never been extinguished or had been kindled afresh to combat this mournful reinvasion of darkness, seemed, in the lawyer's eyes, like a district of some city in a nightmare. The thoughts of his mind, besides, were of the gloomiest dye; and when he glanced at the companion of his drive, he was conscious of some touch of that terror of the law and the law's officers, which may at times assail the most honest.

    As the cab drew up before the address indicated, the fog lifted a little and showed him a dingy street, a gin palace, a low French eating house, a shop for the retail of penny numbers and twopenny salads, many ragged children huddled in the doorways, and many women of many different nationalities passing out, key in hand, to have a morning glass; and the next moment the fog settled down again upon that part, as brown as umber, and cut him off from his blackguardly* surroundings. This was the home of Henry Jekyll's favourite; of a man who was heir to a quarter of a million sterling.

    An ivory-faced and silvery-haired old woman opened the door. She had an evil face, smoothed by hypocrisy: but her manners were excellent. Yes, she said, this was Mr. Hyde's, but he was not at home; he had been in that night very late, but he had gone away again in less than an hour; there was nothing strange in that; his habits were very irregular, and he was often absent; for instance, it was nearly two months since she had seen him till yesterday.

    "Very well, then, we wish to see his rooms," said the lawyer; and when the woman began to declare it was impossible, "I had better tell you who this person is," he added. "This is Inspector Newcomen of Scotland Yard."

    A flash of odious joy appeared upon the woman's face. "Ah!" said she, "he is in trouble! What has he done?"

* *pall* — cloud
* *blackguardly* — dishonourable

Starting with this extract, explore how Stevenson creates a disturbing and threatening atmosphere.

Write about:
- how Stevenson creates a disturbing and threatening atmosphere in this extract
- how Stevenson creates a disturbing and threatening atmosphere in the novella as a whole.

[30 marks]

Your answer may include:

AO1 — show understanding of the text
- Utterson is on his way to apprehend Hyde for brutally murdering Carew. This creates a disturbing and tense atmosphere, since Utterson could be heading to a dangerous situation.
- The dark and ominous weather creates a disturbing and threatening atmosphere. In this extract, it is morning, but the sunlight is shrouded by fog, making it "dark like the back-end of evening". This makes Soho feel unnaturally dark.
- Soho is a poor part of London, full of "ragged children" and "dingy" streets. This contrasts with the luxury and polite society previously described in the novella, and hints that Utterson is somewhere unsafe and unwelcoming.
- Utterson confesses that he feels "terror" towards the police officer who is in the cab with him. This is unsettling as police officers are meant to protect the public.
- Elsewhere in the novella, Dr Lanyon's sudden deterioration and death following a shocking encounter with Jekyll suggests that something is threatening the characters.
- The unprovoked brutality of Hyde's murder of Carew would have been disturbing to readers.

AO2 — show understanding of the writer's language choices
- Stevenson describes how a "chocolate-coloured pall lowered over heaven". This implies that the fog has obscured heaven, implying that God cannot see Soho and that Utterson is beyond God's protection. This is reinforced when Soho is described "like a district of some city in a nightmare". This simile conjures a terrifying image of somewhere almost hellish.
- Foggy weather reoccurs throughout the novella and symbolises how the characters struggle to see what is directly in front of them: Jekyll's true nature.
- The cab "crawled from street to street", which suggests it is moving in a threatening way, like an animal creeping along the ground.

AO3 — relate the novella to the context
- The novella is an example of Gothic fiction. Usually, Gothic fiction is set somewhere remote and mysterious to add to the eerie atmosphere. However, Stevenson chose to set the novella in London. This makes the novella more chilling, as it suggests that transformational science could be happening much closer than readers realise.
- Some Victorian readers were anxious about the end of the century and advancements in science. Stevenson exploits this unease by writing a novella which draws on people's fears.

This answer should be marked in accordance with the levels-based mark scheme on page 53.

> Make sure your answer to this question is in paragraphs and full sentences. Bullet points have been used in this example answer to suggest some information you could include.

CHARACTERS: HASTIE LANYON

Dr Lanyon is good friends with Jekyll and Utterson. He falls out with Jekyll when he disagrees with Jekyll's experiments.

Respected: Utterson calls him *"the great Dr Lanyon"* and his patients are described as *"crowding"* to see him.

Comment: Establishing Lanyon as a respected man of science contrasts with Jekyll's *"scientific heresies"*. Characterising Lanyon as a well-regarded doctor also makes his narrative in Chapter Nine more trustworthy.

Dr Lanyon is a respected man of science.

Healthy: When the reader is first introduced to Lanyon, he is *"hearty, healthy"* and *"red-faced"*.

Comment: Stevenson deliberately describes Lanyon's healthy appearance to make his deterioration in Chapter Six even more pronounced.

Principled: He ends his long friendship with Jekyll over Jekyll's *"unscientific balderdash"*. He's not prepared to associate with someone who pursues *"fanciful"* science.

Comment: Lanyon shuns Jekyll after disagreeing with him over science. This contrasts with Utterson, who stands by Jekyll, even though he is involved with the disreputable Hyde.

Jekyll describes Lanyon as a *"pedant"* in Chapter Three. Jekyll thinks Lanyon's rational and practical view on science is narrow-minded. For more on the theme of science, turn to **page 46**.

Shocked: Watching Hyde transform into Jekyll causes Lanyon to doubt everything he knew about science, and his *"life is shaken to its roots"*.

Comment: Jekyll deliberately chose to reveal the transformation to Lanyon because he may have wanted to prove to Lanyon that his *"fanciful"* experiments worked.

Disturbed: Watching the transformation destroys Lanyon. He is filled with a *"deep-seated terror of mind"* and his physical appearance deteriorates, becoming *"visibly balder and older"*.

Comment: The shock of watching the transformation eventually kills Lanyon. He even comments that he is *"glad to get away"* from living: he doesn't want to exist in a world where Jekyll's experiments are possible.

Lanyon is the only character who sees Hyde transform into Jekyll. This is significant because it proves that the transformation is real: it's not just happening in Jekyll's imagination.

CHARACTERS: RICHARD ENFIELD & POOLE

Mr Enfield is a distant relative of Mr Utterson, and they go walking together every Sunday. Poole is Dr Jekyll's butler.

Mr Enfield

Mr Enfield only appears in Chapters One and Seven.

Secretive: Enfield bumps into Hyde at three o'clock in the morning. This suggests that Enfield may have been out in the middle of the night doing something disreputable.

Comment: Stevenson could be suggesting that most gentlemen had a double life, and that Jekyll wasn't the only character who secretly indulged in sinful behaviour.

Respectable: Outwardly, Enfield is a gentleman who tries to act in an appropriate way. He comes to the rescue of the young girl when Hyde tramples her, and he values discretion: *"the more it looks like Queer Street, the less I ask"*.

Comment: Unlike Utterson, Enfield doesn't interfere when he suspects that Jekyll is involved with Mr Hyde. This could be because Enfield acknowledges that most gentlemen have secrets, so he chooses to turn a blind eye.

Poole

Loyal: Poole has worked for Jekyll for *"twenty years"*.

Comment: Stevenson uses Poole to reveal what happens at Jekyll's house behind closed doors. Poole tells Utterson how Hyde has a key to the laboratory and that Jekyll's servants have been instructed to obey Hyde. This gives the reader insight into how much influence Hyde has over Jekyll's household.

Poole is a household servant, so he is a member of the lower class. Stevenson reflects this in Poole's dialogue. He often speaks more simply than the other characters. He's also referred to by just his surname, rather than Mr Poole.

Concerned: Poole goes to Utterson to ask for help in Chapter Eight because he is *"afraid"* that something might have happened to Jekyll.

Comment: Poole admits that he has been concerned about Jekyll for *"about a week"*. It takes Poole a while to pluck up the courage to ask Utterson for help. This is probably because he was reluctant to go behind Jekyll's back.

THEMES: DUAL NATURE

The novella explores the idea that human behaviour can be contradictory. For example, someone can appear respectable in public, but may behave immorally behind closed doors.

Jekyll and Hyde

From a young age, Jekyll felt the pressure of being *"honourable"*, so he *"concealed"* his *"pleasures"*. Even before Jekyll creates Hyde, he's *"committed to a profound duplicity of life"*.

Comment: Jekyll believes that most people have a dual nature, so he cannot be the only person hiding an evil side. Stevenson could be suggesting that Victorian society was hypocritical: many 'respectable' people probably did bad things behind closed doors.

Jekyll acknowledged that both sides of his personality were *"continuously struggling"*. He wanted to find a way to split his identity so he could have the freedom to do dishonourable things without ruining his reputation.

Comment: Jekyll's desires cause him *"shame"* and make his life *"unbearable"*. Repressing his dark side makes Jekyll so unhappy he's willing to risk death to become Hyde.

Jekyll has a conflicted relationship with Hyde. Jekyll claims that *"It was Hyde... and Hyde alone, that was guilty"* of misdeeds, but he also admits to feeling *"aghast"* by Hyde's actions, and he tries to *"undo the evil done by Hyde"*.

Comment: Jekyll tries to make amends for some of Hyde's behaviour, but he also struggles to admit that Hyde is a part of his identity, and that he is responsible for creating Hyde.

Jekyll sometimes talks about Hyde in the third person, which suggests he is trying to distance himself from Hyde, but sometimes he talks about Hyde in the first person, and acknowledges that they are the same person.

The two sides of Jekyll's identity struggle with each other, and Hyde begins to dominate Jekyll:
- Hyde can take over without drinking the potion.
- It takes a stronger potion for Hyde to transform back into Jekyll.
- Hyde's violence escalates, i.e. murdering Carew.
- Hyde begins to torment Jekyll, i.e. defacing Jekyll's books, pictures and letters.
- Hyde ultimately kills himself, and therefore Jekyll.

Comment: Hyde eventually overpowers Jekyll. Stevenson could be warning his readers about the dangers of giving in to your darkest desires and how evil can overpower goodness.

Some theatre productions of the novella have the same actor play both Jekyll and Hyde. This reinforces the theme of dual nature, and how Jekyll and Hyde share an identity.

Other characters

Stevenson hints that other characters repress their true natures.

Utterson

Utterson wonders with *"envy"* about others' *"misdeeds"*, suggesting that he craves the freedom to do bad things.

Enfield

When Enfield recalls the story of Hyde trampling the girl, he says he was *"coming home from some place at the end of the world, about three o'clock of a black winter morning"*. Enfield is vague about where he has been (*"some place"*) and hints that it is far away from where he lives (*"at the end of the world"*). He's also out very late (*"about three o'clock"*). This seems unusual behaviour and suggests that he could have been doing something disreputable.

The strict nature of Victorian society meant some people concealed their desire to do disreputable things.

Hyde's maid

Stevenson suggests that it's not just the upper classes who have dual natures. Hyde's maid is described as having *"an evil face... but her manners were excellent"*. The juxtaposition of her politeness with her *"evil face"* implies that she is hiding her true nature.

Comment: The reoccurring theme of duality across several characters reinforces the idea that everyone is a mixture of good and evil.

Settings

The novella's settings also reinforce the idea of duality.
- Jekyll's house has a *"great air of wealth and comfort"* but his laboratory at the rear of the house is *"sordid"*.
- Hyde's house in Soho is like *"a district of some city in a nightmare"*. This contrasts with Jekyll's house which has *"the pleasantest room in London"*.
- Sunlight often tries to compete with darkness, which symbolises the struggle between good and evil: *"the fog would be quite broken up, and a haggard shaft of daylight would glance between the swirling wreaths"*.

Comment: Stevenson could be commenting that good and bad will always co-exist, and that you can't have one without the other.

In this extract from the chapter entitled *Henry Jekyll's Full Statement of the Case*, Jekyll describes how he struggled with the good and evil in his personality.

Hence it came about that I concealed my pleasures; and that when I reached years of reflection, and began to look round me and take stock of my progress and position in the world, I stood already committed to a profound duplicity of life. Many a man would have even blazoned such irregularities as I was guilty of; but from the high views that I had set before me, I regarded and hid them with an almost morbid sense of shame. It was thus rather the exacting nature of my aspirations than any particular degradation in my faults, that made me what I was, and, with even a deeper trench than in the majority of men, severed in me those provinces of good and ill which divide and compound man's dual nature. In this case, I was driven to reflect deeply and inveterately* on that hard law of life, which lies at the root of religion and is one of the most plentiful springs of distress. Though so profound a double-dealer, I was in no sense a hypocrite; both sides of me were in dead earnest; I was no more myself when I laid aside restraint and plunged in shame, than when I laboured, in the eye of day, at the furtherance of knowledge or the relief of sorrow and suffering. And it chanced that the direction of my scientific studies, which led wholly towards the mystic and the transcendental, reacted and shed a strong light on this consciousness of the perennial war among my members. With every day, and from both sides of my intelligence, the moral and the intellectual, I thus drew steadily nearer to that truth, by whose partial discovery I have been doomed to such a dreadful shipwreck: that man is not truly one, but truly two. I say two, because the state of my own knowledge does not pass beyond that point. Others will follow, others will outstrip me on the same lines; and I hazard the guess that man will be ultimately known for a mere polity of multifarious, incongruous and independent denizens. I, for my part, from the nature of my life, advanced infallibly in one direction and in one direction only. It was on the moral side, and in my own person, that I learned to recognise the thorough and primitive duality of man; I saw that, of the two natures that contended in the field of my consciousness, even if I could rightly be said to be either, it was only because I was radically both; and from an early date, even before the course of my scientific discoveries had begun to suggest the most naked possibility of such a miracle, I had learned to dwell with pleasure, as a beloved daydream, on the thought of the separation of these elements.

* *inveterately* — habitually

Starting with this extract, explore how Stevenson presents ideas about dual nature in *Strange Case of Dr Jekyll and Mr Hyde*.

Write about:
- how Stevenson presents ideas about dual nature in this extract
- how Stevenson presents ideas about dual nature in the novella as a whole. [30 marks]

Your answer may include:

AO1 — show understanding of the text
- *From a young age, Jekyll struggled with his impulses to do bad things and his desire to maintain a good reputation, so he began to do bad things in private.*
- *Jekyll acknowledges that his "irregularities" weren't that bad, but he put so much pressure on himself to be perfect, he felt a "morbid sense of shame" whenever he did anything wrong. This shows how the two sides to Jekyll's nature have always been in conflict.*
- *Jekyll's solution to his conflicted nature was to split his identity into two so that he could do bad things as Hyde without impacting Jekyll's reputation as an honourable gentleman.*

AO2 — show understanding of the writer's language choices
- *The phrase "perennial war" suggests that the two sides of Jekyll's personality were constantly struggling against each other, which caused him distress and suffering.*
- *Jekyll's language in this extract is full of imagery. He describes splitting his personality as both a "shipwreck" and a "beloved daydream": satisfying his dual nature was both a dream come true and a nightmare.*
- *Jekyll is a scientist, so readers may have expected his language to be factual and precise. However, his use of figurative language suggests he has a creative and imaginative side, reinforcing the idea that his professional image contrasts with this private nature.*

AO3 — relate the novella to the context
- *Stevenson uses Jekyll to show the consequences of a strict, repressive society, where a person's reputation is valued above all else. Jekyll is so ashamed of his behaviour that he would rather split his personality than damage his reputation.*
- *Stevenson also uses Jekyll to highlight how appearances can be deceiving. Outwardly, Jekyll seems to be a respectable gentleman, but he hides a dark secret.*
- *Stevenson also wanted reinforce the idea that most people are a mix of good and bad.*

This answer should be marked in accordance with the levels-based mark scheme on page 53.

Make sure your answer to this question is in paragraphs and full sentences. Bullet points have been used in this example answer to suggest some information you could include.

THEMES: REPUTATION

The characters in the novella go to extreme lengths to protect their reputations.

Jekyll and reputation

Reputation was very important to Victorian gentlemen. Being a gentleman gave a man access to high society and social connections, which could help further his career and status. If a gentleman behaved dishonourably, he risked losing his friends and becoming a social outcast.

Outwardly, Jekyll appears to conform to society's expectations of gentlemanly behaviour:

Being well-mannered, and behaving in a polite way.	Jekyll is described as *"the very pink of the proprieties"*.
Going to church, being a good Christian and avoiding sinful behaviour.	Jekyll is known for his *"charities"* and is *"no less distinguished for religion"*.
Avoiding exaggerated or uncontrolled displays of emotion.	Jekyll wears a *"grave"* (serious) expression in public.
Showing discretion and not gossiping.	When Utterson asks Jekyll about Hyde, Jekyll tells him *"this is a private matter, and I beg of you to let it sleep"*.

Comment: Jekyll feels a lot of pressure to maintain his reputation as a gentleman.

Other characters and reputation

Other characters are also motivated by reputation:

- After witnessing Hyde trample the girl, Enfield threatens to make Hyde's name *"stink from one end of London to the other"*.
- Utterson thinks that Hyde is blackmailing Jekyll over *"the ghost of some old sin"* which could ruin Jekyll's reputation.
- Dr Lanyon distances himself from Jekyll because he doesn't agree with Jekyll's experiments. Lanyon doesn't want his own scientific reputation to be damaged by his association with Jekyll.
- After Carew is murdered, Utterson is worried that Jekyll's name *"might appear"* if there was a murder trial.

Jekyll tries to protect his reputation.

The danger of reputation

Stevenson suggests that focusing too much on reputation can have negative consequences:

- Jekyll goes to extreme lengths to protect his reputation by creating Hyde. As Hyde's control grows, he makes Jekyll *"deathly sick"* and eventually kills him.

- Utterson doesn't force Jekyll to tell him the truth about Hyde, and his honour stops him from reading Lanyon's letter. Utterson's reputation as a gentleman prevents him from finding out the truth before it's too late.

- Jekyll doesn't accept offers of help. He'd rather suffer in silence than risk damaging his (or his friends') reputation.

- Although Jekyll appears to have a good reputation, he is hiding a dark secret. Stevenson could be warning that outward appearances can be deceptive.

- Before he creates Hyde, Jekyll describes his behaviour as *"undignified"*, but Hyde's behaviour escalates to become *"monstrous"*. Stevenson could be warning that repressing your impulses only makes them worse.

In this extract from the chapter entitled *Story of the Door*, Mr Enfield recalls how he witnessed Mr Hyde trampling a young girl in the middle of the night.

"All at once, I saw two figures: one a little man who was stumping along eastward at a good walk, and the other a girl of maybe eight or ten who was running as hard as she was able down a cross street. Well, sir, the two ran into one another naturally enough at the corner; and then came the horrible part of the thing; for the man trampled calmly over the child's body and left her screaming on the ground. It sounds nothing to hear, but it was hellish to see. It wasn't like a man; it was like some damned Juggernaut. I gave a few halloa, took to my heels, collared my gentleman, and brought him back to where there was already quite a group about the screaming child. He was perfectly cool and made no resistance, but gave me one look, so ugly that it brought out the sweat on me like running. The people who had turned out were the girl's own family; and pretty soon, the doctor, for whom she had been sent put in his appearance. Well, the child was not much the worse, more frightened, according to the sawbones; and there you might have supposed would be an end to it. But there was one curious circumstance. I had taken a loathing to my gentleman at first sight. So had the child's family, which was only natural. But the doctor's case was what struck me. He was the usual cut and dry apothecary, of no particular age and colour, with a strong Edinburgh accent and about as emotional as a bagpipe. Well, sir, he was like the rest of us; every time he looked at my prisoner, I saw that sawbones turn sick and white with the desire to kill him. I knew what was in his mind, just as he knew what was in mine; and killing being out of the question, we did the next best. We told the man we could and would make such a scandal out of this as should make his name stink from one end of London to the other. If he had any friends or any credit, we undertook that he should lose them. And all the time, as we were pitching it in red hot, we were keeping the women off him as best we could for they were as wild as harpies. I never saw a circle of such hateful faces; and there was the man in the middle, with a kind of black sneering coolness—frightened too, I could see that—but carrying it off, sir, really like Satan. 'If you choose to make capital out of this accident,' said he, 'I am naturally helpless. No gentleman but wishes to avoid a scene,' says he. 'Name your figure.' Well, we screwed him up to a hundred pounds for the child's family; he would have clearly liked to stick out; but there was something about the lot of us that meant mischief, and at last he struck. The next thing was to get the money; and where do you think he carried us but to that place with the door?—whipped out a key, went in, and presently came back with the matter of ten pounds in gold and a cheque for the balance on Coutts's, drawn payable to bearer and signed with a name that I can't mention, though it's one of the points of my story, but it was a name at least very well known and often printed."

Starting with this extract, explore how Stevenson presents ideas about reputation in *Strange Case of Dr Jekyll and Mr Hyde*.

Write about:
- how Stevenson presents ideas about reputation in this extract
- how Stevenson presents ideas about reputation in the novella as a whole. [30 marks]

Your answer may include:

AO1 — show understanding of the text
- *Enfield is obliged to intervene because, as a gentleman, helping the trampled child would be the honourable thing to do.*
- *Enfield thinks damaging Hyde's reputation is the "next best" thing to killing him, showing how much importance was placed on reputation.*
- *This extract is ironic. The reader later discovers that Hyde doesn't care about his reputation, but he's prepared to pay £100 (a considerable sum in the 19th century) to avoid bringing any attention to himself that could prevent him from committing misdeeds.*
- *Enfield tries to be discreet about who signed the cheque to protect their reputation ("a name that I can't mention").*
- *Enfield and Utterson stroll through London weekly, reminding others of their position in society.*
- *Jekyll creates Hyde so that he can do sinful things without damaging his reputation.*

AO2 — show understanding of the writer's language choices
- *This extract was taken from the opening chapter. Introducing the theme of reputation so early in the novella emphasises its importance to the story.*
- *Enfield uses the word "sir" when talking to Utterson. This was a mark of respect, and reflects the polite way that gentlemen spoke to each other at the time.*
- *The phrase "make his name stink from one end of London to the other" suggests that gossip about a person's misdeeds could spread across the capital, showing that Londoners put a lot of emphasis on reputation. The verb "stink" suggests that people would turn away from Hyde like they would a bad smell.*

AO3 — relate the novella to the context
- *Stevenson uses Jekyll to show how Victorian society forced people to do undignified things in secret to protect their reputations. Stevenson could be warning that repressing these impulses only intensifies them and makes them worse.*
- *Stevenson could be suggesting that outward appearances can be deceptive. Although Jekyll seems like a gentleman, he's hiding a monstrous side.*
- *Stevenson publicly enjoyed a bohemian lifestyle that gave him greater freedom. He rejected expectations about socially acceptable behaviour.*

This answer should be marked in accordance with the levels-based mark scheme on page 53.

> ⭐ Make sure your answer to this question is in paragraphs and full sentences. Bullet points have been used in this example answer to suggest some information you could include.

THEMES: RELIGION AND SCIENCE

In the 19th century, religion and science were often at odds with one another.

Religion and science in the 19th century

In the late Victorian period, most people in Britain were Christians who attended church and believed what was taught in the Bible. However, new scientific discoveries began to undermine some religious teachings. For example, Charles Darwin (see **page 5**) theorised that humans had evolved from apes. His theory contradicted the Christian belief that God created mankind, so Darwin's theory caused divisions in society: it led some to question their faith, while others ridiculed Darwin and rejected his ideas altogether.

Comment: Scientific advancements in the Victorian era made some people anxious because they were worried what impact science might have on their lives and how it might challenge religion. Stevenson exploits this unease by highlighting how science can be used for evil and immoral purposes.

Although many saw Christianity as a force for good that encouraged charity and forgiveness, the novella also hints that religion can contribute to a repressive society. Stevenson implies that many people in the Victorian era felt under pressure to lead moral, sin-free lives, and were encouraged to criticise those who behave sinfully.

Stevenson was an atheist (someone who doesn't believe in the existence of God).

Hyde and religion

In the novella, Hyde was not created by God, but by man's wickedness. As such, he is presented as evil and unnatural. Stevenson uses language associated with the Devil to reinforce this. For example, Hyde is described as *"damned"* with *"Satan's signature"* on his face.

When Jekyll loses control of Hyde, Hyde scribbles *"startling blasphemies"* (words which disrespect God) over a religious text. This further connects Hyde with the Devil, implying that Hyde not only rejects Christianity, but hates it.

Comment: Renouncing religion would have been shocking to Victorian readers.

Jekyll and religion

Jekyll is a Christian: *"whilst he had always been known for charities, he was now no less distinguished for religion"*. However, behind closed doors he is *"the chief of sinners"*.

Comment: Stevenson highlights the hypocrisy of some Christians: they can outwardly appear religious, but are *"secret sinners"* in private.

Jekyll and science

Comment: Stevenson uses technical language to make the science in the novella seem more realistic, for example, *"effervesce"*, *"vapour"*, *"ebullition"* and *"compound"*.

Jekyll's science is described as *"transcendental"* (spiritual) and *"mystic"* which suggests he is experimenting with the supernatural. This contrasts with typical science which focuses on the real world, using logic and rational thought.

Stevenson presents Jekyll's science negatively:
- Lanyon was so upset by Jekyll's *"fanciful"* science it caused the men to stop talking to each other.
- Jekyll's laboratory was once used for dissections, which links his science with death.
- His laboratory is untidy: *"the floor strewn with crates and littered with packing straw"*. This suggests that Jekyll's science is messy and frenzied, not careful and precise.
- Jekyll has evil intentions, so his experiments produce a *"fiend"* rather than an *"angel"*.

Jekyll's science is controversial.

Comment: Stevenson warns about the dangers of science, suggesting that if it is used for evil purposes it can lead to a person's downfall.

Lanyon and religion

When Hyde visits Lanyon, he gives Lanyon the option to watch him drink the potion. Hyde tempts Lanyon, telling him that watching will bring him *"new avenues of fame and power"*. This has parallels with the story of Adam and Eve, and links Hyde with the serpent who tempts Eve. In both examples, the *"greed of curiosity"* causes their downfall.

Adam and Eve lived in paradise called the Garden of Eden. However, a serpent tempted Eve to eat fruit from the Tree of Knowledge, something she had been forbidden from doing. As a result, Adam and Eve were banished from Eden, and sent to Earth as punishment.

Lanyon and science

Foils are characters who share some similarities, but make different choices. Writers use foils to reveal information about one character by contrasting their behaviour and emotions with another.

Lanyon acts as a **foil** to Jekyll. Like Jekyll, Lanyon is a doctor, but unlike Jekyll, he uses his scientific knowledge for good, by treating the sick. This contrasts with Jekyll who uses his knowledge for evil purposes.

In this extract from the chapter entitled *Dr Lanyon's Narrative*, Hyde visits Dr Lanyon and creates a potion which turns him into Jekyll.

    He thanked me with a smiling nod, measured out a few minims of the red tincture and added one of the powders. The mixture, which was at first of a reddish hue, began, in proportion as the crystals melted, to brighten in colour, to effervesce audibly, and to throw off small fumes of vapour. Suddenly and at the same moment, the ebullition ceased and the compound changed to a dark purple, which faded again more slowly to a watery green. My visitor, who had watched these metamorphoses with a keen eye, smiled, set down the glass upon the table, and then turned and looked upon me with an air of scrutiny.

    "And now," said he, "to settle what remains. Will you be wise? Will you be guided? Will you suffer me to take this glass in my hand and to go forth from your house without further parley? Or has the greed of curiosity too much command of you? Think before you answer, for it shall be done as you decide. As you decide, you shall be left as you were before, and neither richer nor wiser, unless the sense of service rendered to a man in mortal distress may be counted as a kind of riches of the soul. Or, if you shall so prefer to choose, a new province of knowledge and new avenues to fame and power shall be laid open to you, here, in this room, upon the instant; and your sight shall be blasted by a prodigy to stagger the unbelief of Satan."

    "Sir," said I, affecting a coolness that I was far from truly possessing, "you speak enigmas, and you will perhaps not wonder that I hear you with no very strong impression of belief. But I have gone too far in the way of inexplicable services to pause before I see the end."

    "It is well," replied my visitor. "Lanyon, you remember your vows: what follows is under the seal of our profession. And now, you who have so long been bound to the most narrow and material views, you who have denied the virtue of transcendental medicine, you who have derided your superiors—behold!"

    He put the glass to his lips and drank at one gulp. A cry followed; he reeled, staggered, clutched at the table and held on, staring with injected eyes, gasping with open mouth; and as I looked there came, I thought, a change—he seemed to swell—his face became suddenly black and the features seemed to melt and alter—and the next moment, I had sprung to my feet and leaped back against the wall, my arms raised to shield me from that prodigy, my mind submerged in terror.

    "O God!" I screamed, and "O God!" again and again; for there before my eyes—pale and shaken, and half fainting, and groping before him with his hands, like a man restored from death— there stood Henry Jekyll!

Starting with this extract, explore how Stevenson presents ideas about science and religion.

Write about:
- how Stevenson presents ideas about science and religion in this extract.
- how Stevenson presents ideas about science and religion in the novella as a whole. [30 marks]

Your answer may include:

AO1 — show understanding of the text
- Hyde tempts Lanyon with a sight that will bring him "new avenues to fame and power". This has parallels with the story of Adam and Eve from the Bible, suggesting that Jekyll is tempting Lanyon with scientific knowledge like the serpent in the Garden of Eden tempting Eve with the fruit of knowledge. This suggests that Jekyll's science is evil and sinful.
- Lanyon appeals to God after watching the transformation because he has seen something unnatural and unholy, and wants God to protect him. Since Lanyon is presented elsewhere as a rational, logical doctor, this desperate plea shows just how frightened he is.
- Earlier in the novella, Lanyon and Jekyll disagree over science. Jekyll may have chosen to transform in front of Lanyon as proof that his science is not "fanciful" or "balderdash".
- Elsewhere in the novella, Jekyll is presented as a good Christian, whereas Hyde rejects religion. Hyde scribbles "blasphemies" across Jekyll's religious texts.

AO2 — show understanding of the writer's language choices
- This extract is told from Lanyon's perspective. Stevenson uses technical language to emphasise his scientific background, e.g. "tincture", "effervesce", "ebullition".
- The phrase "stagger the unbelief of Satan" suggests that Jekyll's science is associated with the Devil. This is reinforced by the description of the transformation which uses visceral language to show its unpleasantness. For example, during the transformation Hyde is described as swelling and melting, and this disturbing image reinforces how unnatural and unholy Jekyll's science is.

AO3 — relate the novella to the context
- In the 19th century, Darwin theorised that mankind was evolved from apes. Hyde is often compared to animals, often monkeys or apes. This characterises Hyde as sub-human and less evolved. Darwin's theory was controversial, as it contradicted the Biblical theory of creationism. It caused a division between science and religion, as some Victorians began to reject religious explanations while others mocked scientific explanations.
- Scientific advancements in the Victorian period made some people feel anxious and uneasy about the future. Stevenson exploits this feeling of unease by suggesting that science can be used for evil and immoral purposes.
- Stevenson was an atheist, and he uses the novella to criticise religion. He uses Jekyll to suggest that some people who claimed to be good Christians were actually "secret sinners" and that many religious people were hypocritical.

This answer should be marked in accordance with the levels-based mark scheme on page 53.

> Make sure your answer to this question is in paragraphs and full sentences. Bullet points have been used in this example answer to suggest some information you could include.

GCSE English Literature | Dr Jekyll and Mr Hyde

THEMES: SECRECY

Most of the characters are keeping secrets from one another.

Jekyll

Stevenson uses Jekyll to warn readers about the dangers of secretive behaviour. From a young age, Jekyll *"concealed [his] pleasures"*, which he describes as *"undignified"*. He goes to great lengths to secretly indulge in immoral behaviour by creating Hyde. However, Hyde worsens Jekyll's secretive nature because his behaviour escalates from *"undignified"* to *"monstrous"*.

Comment: Stevenson could be saying that people should be more accepting of people's faults. If people are forced to hide their wrongdoings because they are fearful of judgement, it will only make the situation worse.

Secrets

Several characters keep secrets from Utterson. These secrets are an important dramatic device, as they create suspense for the reader and misdirect Utterson.

Enfield	In Chapter One, Enfield refuses to tell Utterson who signed Hyde's cheque.
Jekyll	In Chapter Two, Jekyll won't tell Utterson how he's involved with Hyde.
Lanyon	In Chapter Six, Lanyon won't tell Utterson what shocking thing he witnessed which has caused him to prematurely age. He also won't explain why he won't talk to Jekyll anymore.

Comment: Lanyon and Jekyll are only prepared to reveal the truth when they're close to death.

These secrets cause Utterson to jump to the wrong conclusion. He initially assumes that Hyde is blackmailing Jekyll, and later believes that Jekyll's odd behaviour is due to a mysterious illness.

Symbolism and secrecy

Weather

The weather in the novella is often foggy. This symbolises secrecy, and how it's difficult for the characters to uncover the truth about Hyde.

Jekyll's door

In Chapter Eight, Poole and Utterson destroy Jekyll's door to get into his cabinet. It's only when the door is broken that the characters discover what has happened.

EXAMINATION PRACTICE

> In this extract from the chapter entitled *Dr Jekyll was Quite at Ease*, Utterson and Jekyll discuss Jekyll's will.
>
> *"I have been wanting to speak to you, Jekyll,"* began the latter. *"You know that will of yours?"*
>
> *A close observer might have gathered that the topic was distasteful; but the doctor carried it off gaily. "My poor Utterson," said he, "you are unfortunate in such a client. I never saw a man so distressed as you were by my will; unless it were that hide-bound pedant, Lanyon, at what he called my scientific heresies. O, I know he's a good fellow—you needn't frown—an excellent fellow, and I always mean to see more of him; but a hide-bound pedant for all that; an ignorant, blatant pedant. I was never more disappointed in any man than Lanyon."*
>
> *"You know I never approved of it,"* pursued Utterson, ruthlessly disregarding the fresh topic.
>
> *"My will? Yes, certainly, I know that,"* said the doctor, a trifle sharply. *"You have told me so."*
>
> *"Well, I tell you so again,"* continued the lawyer. *"I have been learning something of young Hyde."*
>
> *The large handsome face of Dr. Jekyll grew pale to the very lips, and there came a blackness about his eyes. "I do not care to hear more," said he. "This is a matter I thought we had agreed to drop."*
>
> *"What I heard was abominable,"* said Utterson.
>
> *"It can make no change. You do not understand my position,"* returned the doctor, with a certain incoherency of manner. *"I am painfully situated, Utterson; my position is a very strange—a very strange one. It is one of those affairs that cannot be mended by talking."*
>
> *"Jekyll,"* said Utterson, *"you know me: I am a man to be trusted. Make a clean breast of this in confidence; and I make no doubt I can get you out of it."*
>
> *"My good Utterson,"* said the doctor, *"this is very good of you, this is downright good of you, and I cannot find words to thank you in. I believe you fully; I would trust you before any man alive, ay, before myself, if I could make the choice; but indeed it isn't what you fancy; it is not as bad as that; and just to put your good heart at rest, I will tell you one thing: the moment I choose, I can be rid of Mr. Hyde. I give you my hand upon that; and I thank you again and again; and I will just add one little word, Utterson, that I'm sure you'll take in good part: this is a private matter, and I beg of you to let it sleep."*

Starting with extract, explore how Stevenson presents secrecy in *Strange Case of Dr Jekyll and Mr Hyde*.

Write about:
- how Stevenson presents secrecy in this extract
- how Stevenson presents secrecy in the novella as a whole. [30 marks]

EXAMINATION PRACTICE ANSWERS

Strange Case of Dr Jekyll and Mr Hyde is an example of Gothic fiction, a genre of literature which was incredibly popular in the 19th century. Gothic fiction is notable for its sense of foreboding and mystery, and one way this is achieved is by hinting at secrets which keep the reader in suspense until they are revealed. Throughout the novella, the reasons for Jekyll's secretive behaviour and his mysterious connection with Mr Hyde are not resolved until the final chapter. By maintaining these secrets, Stevenson keeps his readers on the edge of their seats until the very end. The supernatural nature of this secret also creates an unforgettable twist, which leads to a disturbing and uneasy conclusion.

In this extract, Utterson is concerned that his friend is secretly being blackmailed by Hyde, so Utterson presses Jekyll about two matters: Jekyll's unusual will, and his connection with the disreputable Mr Hyde. Mentioning the will is *"distasteful"* and ungentlemanly, but Utterson is determined to understand how his friend is involved with Hyde. However, Jekyll is keeping a shocking secret from Utterson, and he refuses to confess the truth about Hyde. Despite this, Stevenson includes hints in Jekyll's language and appearance that almost betray his secret.

Firstly, Jekyll tries to distract Utterson from asking about his will by bringing up his falling out with Lanyon. However, Jekyll's language is quite revealing. He calls Lanyon a *"hide-bound pendant"*, comparing Lanyon and his conservative scientific views to an old-fashioned, tightly wrapped leather book. However, this phrase sounds like 'Hyde-bound', which is ironic, because Jekyll is bound by the actions of his alter-ego, Mr Hyde.

Secondly, when Utterson tries to broach the subject of Hyde, a physical change comes over Jekyll, and there is a *"blackness about his eyes"*. This blackness could be interpreted as Hyde lurking inside Jekyll, as earlier in the novella, Hyde is described as having a *"black sneering coolness"*. This emphasises how Hyde is an inescapable part of Jekyll who resides within him.

Elsewhere in the novella, characters keep secrets and withhold information from Utterson. This allows Stevenson to maintain suspense. For example, Dr Lanyon never reveals the *"scientific heresies"* that have caused him to stop talking to Jekyll, and Lanyon doesn't reveal the shock he has witnessed that has brought him close to death. These secrets are an important dramatic device as they create a sense of tension and foreboding which build until Utterson breaks down Jekyll's door with an axe.

The truth about Jekyll's relationship with Hyde is only revealed in the final two chapters, which means that readers are kept in suspense for almost the entirety of the novella. Jekyll is only prepared to admit to his connection with Hyde when he knows that his life is almost over. This shows the extreme lengths that Jekyll is prepared to go to keep his connection to Hyde a secret.

Stevenson could be warning his readers about the dangers of secrets. If Jekyll had confided in Utterson sooner, the deaths of Carew, Lanyon and Jekyll may have been avoided. However, Stevenson shows how repressive Victorian society forces people to behave secretly to protect their reputations with disastrous consequences.

LEVELS-BASED MARK SCHEMES FOR EXTENDED RESPONSE QUESTIONS

Questions that require extended writing use mark bands. The whole answer will be marked together to determine which mark band it fits into, and which mark should be awarded within the mark band.

The descriptors below have been written in simple language to give an indication of the expectations of each mark band. See the AQA website for the official mark schemes used.

Level	Students' answers tend to...
6 (26–30 marks)	<ul><li>Focus on the text as conscious construct (i.e. a novella written by Stevenson intended to have a deliberate effect).</li><li>Produce a logical and well-structured response which closely uses the text to explore their argument / interpretation.</li><li>Analyse the writer's craft by considering the effects of a writer's choice, linked closely to meanings.</li><li>Understand the writer's purpose and context.</li></ul>
5 (21–25 marks)	<ul><li>Start to think about ideas in a more developed way.</li><li>Think about the deeper meaning of a text and start to explore alternative interpretations.</li><li>Start to focus on specific elements of writer's craft, linked to meanings.</li><li>Focus more on abstract concepts, such as themes and ideas, than narrative events or character feelings.</li></ul>
4 (16–20 marks)	<ul><li>Sustain a focus on an idea, or a particular technique.</li><li>Start to consider how the text works and what the writer is doing.</li><li>Use examples effectively to support their points.</li><li>Explain the effect of a writer's method on the text, with a clear focus on it having been consciously written.</li><li>Show an understanding of ideas and themes.</li></ul>
3 (11–15 marks)	<ul><li>Explain their ideas.</li><li>Demonstrate knowledge of the text as a whole.</li><li>Show awareness of the concept of themes.</li><li>Identify the effects of a range of methods on the reader.</li></ul>
2 (6–10 marks)	<ul><li>Support their comments by using references to / from the text.</li><li>Make comments that are generally relevant to the question.</li><li>Identify at least one method and possibly make some comment on the effect of it on the reader</li></ul>
1 (1–5 marks)	<ul><li>Describe the text.</li><li>Retell the narrative.</li><li>Make references to, rather than use references from, the text.</li></ul>
0 marks	Nothing worthy of credit / nothing written.

INDEX

19th-century writing style 8

A
Adam and Eve 23, 29, 47
alliteration 10
ambiguous language 7, 15
Assessment Objectives vi
atheism 2, 46

B
blackmail 12–14
bohemianism 2

C
chapters 6
Charles Darwin 5, 46
class 4
cliff-hanger 7, 14, 16
creationism 5, 46

D
Danvers Carew 16, 26
Darwin, Charles 5, 46
detective novel 2
dramatic irony 33
drug addiction 26
dual nature 24, 26, 38, 39

E
Enfield 6, 11, 12, 19, 37, 39, 50
epistolary form 3, 6
exclamations 9

F
fin de siècle 5

G
gentlemen 4, 12, 23, 28, 32, 42
Gothic fiction 2, 3, 7, 33

H
Hyde 11–17, 21– 26, 28, 29, 38, 46
Hyde's maid 39

J
Jekyll 6, 8, 15, 17–21, 23–28, 38, 46, 47, 50

L
laboratory 14, 17, 19, 20
language techniques 8, 9, 10
Lanyon 8, 13, 18, 22, 23, 36, 47, 50
letters 6, 17, 18, 21, 22, 24
London 3, 4

M
maid 16
metaphors 10
Mr Guest 17

N
narrator 6

P
pathetic fallacy 10
personification 10
physiognomy 24
Poole 14, 17, 20, 21, 37
protagonist 27

R
religion 5, 46, 47
reputation 12, 27, 28, 42, 43
rhetorical questions 9, 22
Robert Louis Stevenson 2

S
science 13, 23, 27, 36, 46, 47
secrecy 27, 50
semantic field 10
sensory language 9
setting 4, 39
similes 10
Stevenson, Robert Louis 2
structure 6
symbolism 9, 21, 50

T
tension 7, 14
Theory of Evolution 5, 29

U
Utterson 6, 8, 11–15, 17–21, 32, 33, 39

W
weather 3, 16, 20, 50

ACKNOWLEDGMENTS

The questions in this ClearRevise guide are the sole responsibility of the authors and have neither been provided nor approved by the examination board.

Every effort has been made to trace and acknowledge ownership of copyright. The publishers will be happy to make any future amendments with copyright owners that it has not been possible to contact. The publisher would like to thank the following companies and individuals who granted permission for the use of their images in this textbook.

Page 2 — Robert Louis Stevenson © Pictorial Press Ltd / Alamy Stock Photo

Page 4 — Fashionable Men 1857 © Chronicle / Alamy Stock Photo

Page 5 — Cartoon of Charles Darwin 1871 © FineArt / Alamy Stock Photo

Page 7 — Jekyll and Hyde poster © Everett Collection / Shutterstock.com

Page 8 — Photo by Mark Douet

Page 11 — Dr Jekyll and Mr Hyde 1931 © Masheter Movie Archive / Alamy Stock Photo

Page 14 — © Alex Harvey-Brown

Page 15 — Photo by Mark Douet

Page 16 — © Alex Harvey-Brown

Page 17 — Photo by Mark Douet

Page 19 — © Alex Harvey-Brown

Page 23 — Photo by Mark Douet

Page 25 — © Alex Harvey-Brown

Page 27 — © Alex Harvey-Brown

Page 28 — Photo by Mark Douet

Page 29 — Dr Jekyll and Mr Hyde, Paramount 1931 © Granger - Historical Picture Archive / Alamy Stock Photo

Page 32 — © Alex Harvey-Brown

Page 33 — Photo by Mark Douet

Page 36 — © Alex Harvey-Brown

Page 39 — Billy Rose Theatre Division, The New York Public Library. "Richard Mansfield" The New York Public Library Digital Collections. 1850 - 2020. https://digitalcollections.nypl.org/items/510d47de-8e24-a3d9-e040-e00a18064a99

Page 42 — Photo by Mark Douet

Page 47 — Photo by Mark Douet

All other photographs and graphics © Shutterstock.

NOTES, DOODLES AND EXAM DATES

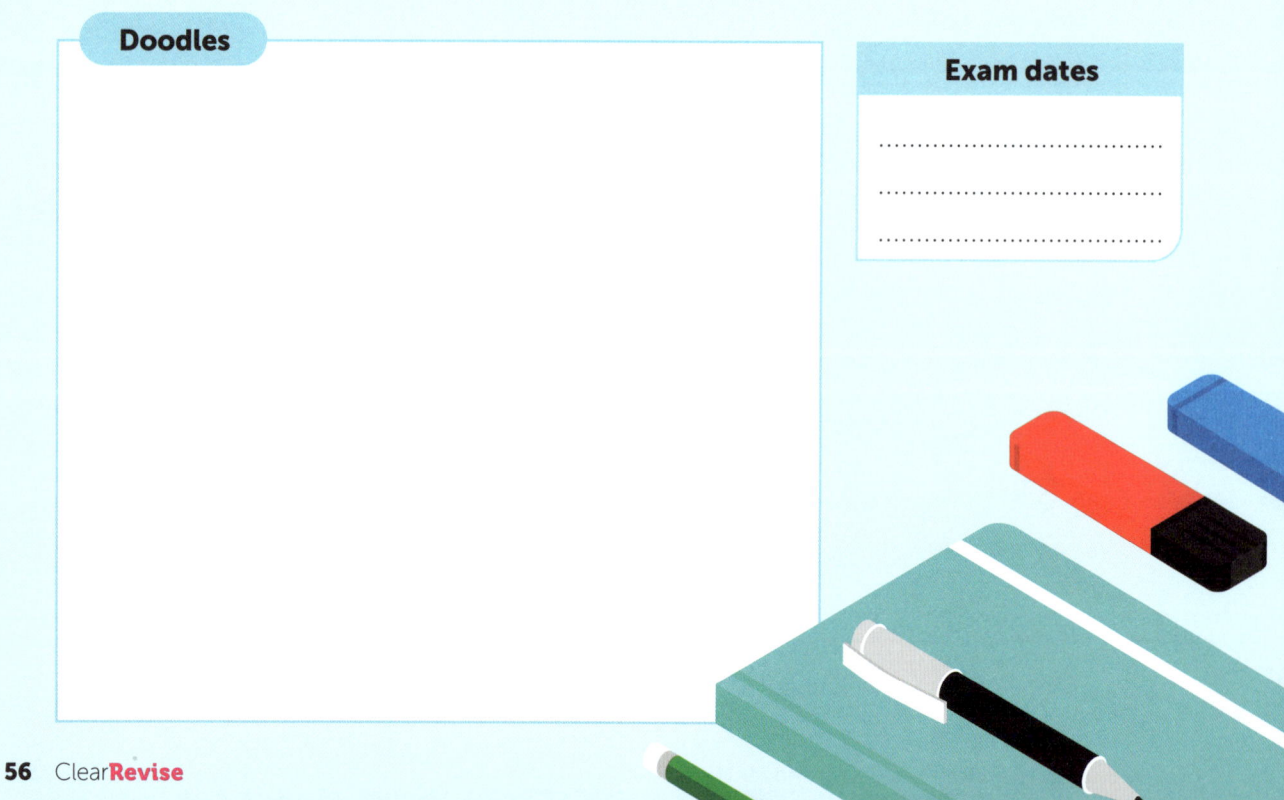

Doodles

Exam dates

EXAMINATION TIPS

With your examination practice, use a boundary approximation using the following table. Be aware that the grade boundaries can vary from year to year, so they should be used as a guide only.

Grade	9	8	7	6	5	4	3	2	1
Boundary	88%	79%	71%	61%	52%	43%	31%	21%	10%

1. Read the question carefully. Don't give an answer to a question that you *think* is appearing (or wish was appearing!) rather than the actual question.
2. Spend time reading through the extract, and think about what happens before and after, and how it links to other parts of the novella. The statement above the extract will help you identify where in the novella it is from.
3. It's worth jotting down a quick plan to make sure your answer includes sufficient detail and is focused on the question.
4. The question will ask you about the extract and the novella as a whole, but you don't need to spend an equal amount of time on both. If you're struggling to make close textual references about the extract, you can concentrate on the rest of the novella instead.
5. Start your answer with a brief introduction where you summarise the main points of your response. This can help your answer to stay on-track.
6. A discussion of Stevenson's methods can include his language choices, but also structural choices (such as the ordering of events), how characters develop, and what their actions tell you about their characterisation.
7. Include details from the text to support your answer. These details might be quotes, or they can be references to the text.
8. Make sure your handwriting is legible. The examiner can't award you marks if they can't read what you've written.
9. The examiner will be impressed if you can correctly use technical terms like 'dramatic irony', 'metaphor', 'personification' etc, but to get the best marks you need to explore the effect of these techniques.
10. Use linking words and phrases to show you are developing your points or comparing information, for example, "this reinforces", "this shows that" and "on the other hand". This helps to give your answer structure and makes it easier for the examiner to award you marks.
11. If you need extra paper, make sure you clearly signal that your answer is continued elsewhere. Remember that longer answers don't necessarily score more highly than shorter, more concise answers.

Good luck!

Revision, re-imagined

These guides are everything you need to ace your exams and beam with pride. Each topic is laid out in a beautifully illustrated format that is clear, approachable and as concise and simple as possible.

They have been expertly compiled and edited by subject specialists, highly experienced examiners, industry professionals and a good dollop of scientific research into what makes revision most effective. Past examination questions are essential to good preparation, improving understanding and confidence.

- Hundreds of marks worth of examination style questions
- Answers provided for all questions within the books
- Illustrated topics to improve memory and recall
- Specification references for every topic
- Examination tips and techniques
- Free Python solutions pack (CS Only)

Absolute clarity is the aim.

Explore the series and add to your collection at **www.clearrevise.com**

Available from all good book shops

amazon   @pgonlinepub

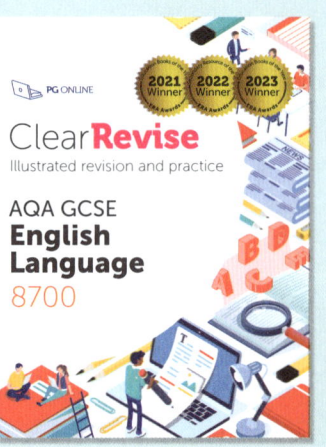

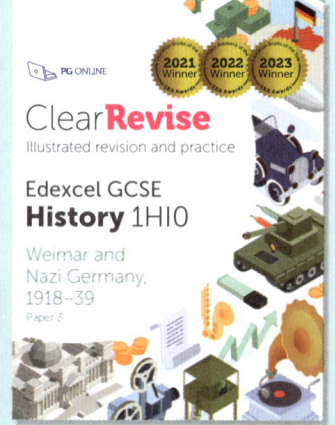

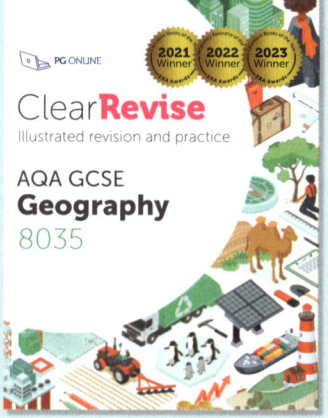

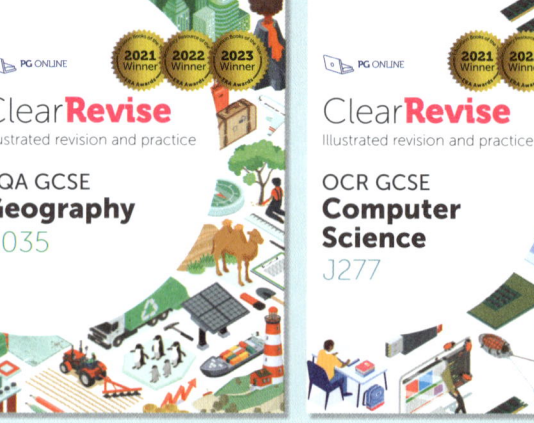

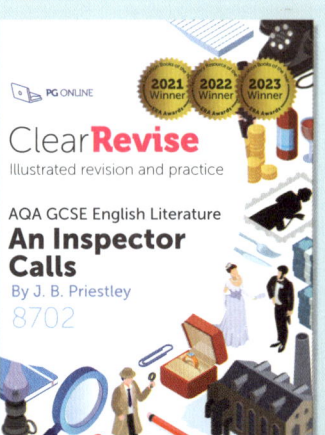

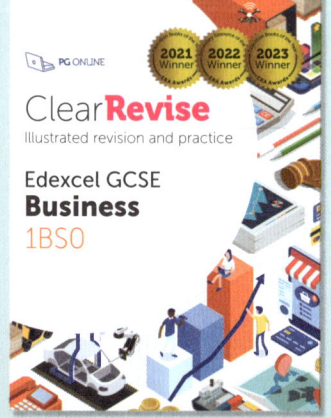

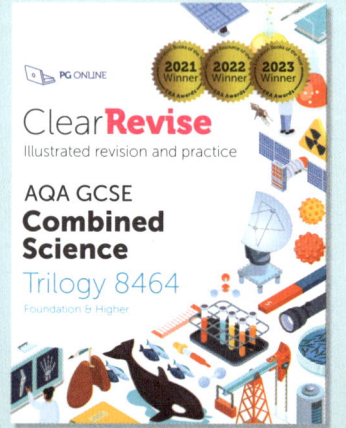

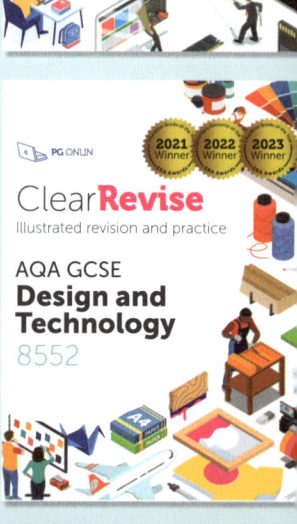

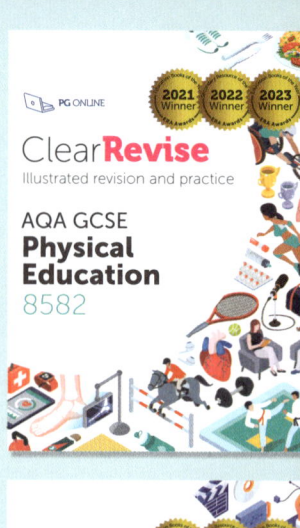

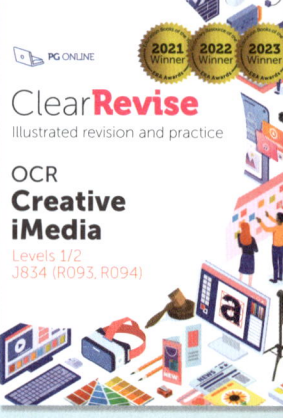

New titles coming soon!

ClearRevise titles:
- AQA GCSE Physical Education 8582
- OCR Creative iMedia Levels 1/2 J834 (R093, R094)
- AQA GCSE English Language 8700
- Edexcel GCSE History 1HI0 — Weimar and Nazi Germany, 1918–39 Paper 3
- AQA GCSE Geography 8035
- OCR GCSE Computer Science J277
- AQA GCSE English Literature — An Inspector Calls By J. B. Priestley 8702
- Edexcel GCSE Business 1BS0
- AQA GCSE Combined Science Trilogy 8464 Foundation & Higher
- AQA GCSE Design and Technology 8552